British Imperial History

Simon J. Potter

 macmillan
education palgrave

First published 2015 by
PALGRAVE

Palgrave in the UK is an imprint of Macmillan Publishers Limited, registered in England, company number 785998, of 4 Crinan Street, London N1 9XW.

Palgrave Macmillan in the US is a division of St Martin's Press LLC, 175 Fifth Avenue, New York, NY 10010.

Palgrave is a global imprint of the above companies and is represented throughout the world.

Palgrave® and Macmillan® are registered trademarks in the United States, the United Kingdom, Europe and other countries.

ISBN 978–1–137–34183–9   hardback
ISBN 978–1–137–34182–2   paperback

This book is printed on paper suitable for recycling and made from fully managed and sustained forest sources. Logging, pulping and manufacturing processes are expected to conform to the environmental regulations of the country of origin.

A catalogue record for this book is available from the British Library.

A catalog record for this book is available from the Library of Congress.

Typeset by MPS Limited, Chennai, India.

Printed in China

British Imp   **Z954734**

Why did the British ⟨e⟩mpire expand so dramatically in the late eighteenth and nineteenth centuries – and why did it then collapse so rapidly after the Second World War? Drawing on the latest scholarship from around the world, *British Imperial History* provides a clear, critical survey of the major concepts and theories used by historians of the modern British empire.

British Imperial History:

- brings together in a single volume the key ideas used by political, economic, social and cultural historians, using a theoretical rather than a narrative approach
- examines debates from the origins of British imperialism to decolonization
- includes a chapter on the recent academic turn towards global history.

This informative guide to the historiography of the British empire is essential for all students of the topic, and is equally useful for those studying historical approaches in general.

Simon J. Potter is Reader in Modern History at the University of Bristol, UK, where his research focuses on media and the British empire.

Theory and History
Series Editor: Donald MacRaild

Published

Biography and History	*Barbara Caine*
Film and History	*James Chapman*
Empiricism and History	*Stephen Davies*
Cultural History	*Anna Green*
Gender and History	*Susan Kingsley Kent*
Social Theory and Social History	*Donald M. MacRaild and Avram Taylor*
Narrative and History	*Alun Munslow*
Marxism and History	*Matt Perry*
British Imperial History	*Simon J. Potter*
Transnational History	*Pierre-Yves Saunier*
Postmodernism and History	*Willie Thompson*

Theory and History
Series Standing Order
ISBN 978–1–4039–8526–2 hardback
ISBN 978–0–333–91921–7 paperback
(*outside North America only*)

You can receive future titles in this series as they are published. To place a standing order please contact your bookseller or, in the case of difficulty, write to us at the address below with your name and address, the title of the series and the ISBN quoted above.

Customer Services Department, Macmillan Distribution Ltd,
Houndmills, Basingstoke, Hampshire, RG21 6XS, UK

For Maria

Contents

Preface

This book offers an introduction to some of the key concepts and theories encountered when studying the history of the British empire. It seeks to show how those concepts and theories relate to the broader approaches to writing history – economic, political, social, and cultural – that characterize the discipline. I hope it will be of use both to students of the British empire and to those thinking about how we approach the study of history more generally.

Rather than offering 'readings' of abstract philosophical or critical theoretical works – these are already available in many other places – this book looks at how different historians of empire have deployed theories and concepts, and at the strengths and weaknesses of those analytical structures. It focuses on the nineteenth and twentieth centuries, but also glances back to the origins of British power in eighteenth-century India, one of the vital foundations for the British world-system that endured until after the Second World War.

Few of the theories and concepts developed by imperial historians are uncontroversial, and the book traces some of the historiographical debates that these ideas have generated. Controversy enlivens and stimulates research, makes or breaks academic reputations, and provides fertile ground for the cultivation of essay questions. Yet it can also conceal significant areas of consensus and continuity in history writing. I have thus also sought to convey how, for all the sound and fury of historiographical debate, older and newer approaches to writing the history of the British empire are often complementary. Scholars sometimes exaggerate the antagonism between different types of history writing, or refuse to engage seriously with histories written from a perspective other than their own. Nevertheless, when taken together, their diverse efforts have brought us some way toward a holistic understanding of the history of the British empire, engaging with the topic on a very broad front. The types of questions that historians of empire can now seek to answer are more varied than ever before, and the range is set to become wider still as new research branches out into areas such as medical history, the history of psychiatry, environmental history, and animal history.

Recently I have sharpened my understanding of the issues discussed in Chapter 5 through discussion and collaboration with my colleague, Jonathan Saha. I have wrestled with many of the other theories and concepts discussed in this book since my time as a graduate student at the University of Oxford, and while researching and teaching at the National University of Ireland, Galway, and the University of Bristol. Students, colleagues, and friends, too numerous to mention individually, have shaped my understanding of the subject. Thank you. I owe a special debt of gratitude to Ged Martin who, as always, offered much sage advice as I wrote this book.

The book is dedicated to my wife, Maria Scott, with love.

Introduction

▶ **Questions and approaches**

Why did the British empire expand? Why did it collapse? Who, and what, drove the making of imperial policies? How was the British empire ruled? How did it change the societies that it sprang from, encountered, and incorporated? Was it a 'world-shaping force', transforming economies, societies, and cultures in Britain and its colonies? How far did empire strengthen and create divisions of class, race, and gender? How did the British empire interact with and reshape the wider, global systems of trade and power of which it was a part? These are all obvious and fundamental questions, and historians have grappled with them for decades. Yet they have seldom been able to agree on definitive answers to any of them.

This quarrelsomeness reflects one of the most obvious characteristics of the discipline of history more generally: when historians debate the big issues, we seldom reach any sort of consensus. This is in part a product of the nature of the historical method of enquiry. Typically, historians work alone or in pairs, carrying out research into relatively limited areas of our chosen field. We work in archives of one sort or another, collect evidence, and offer interpretations based on that evidence. But what happens when we try to make the leap from empirical research concerning individual examples to assembling an overall pattern? What is the aggregated meaning of all our varied case studies? How does the work of each historian relate to the findings of others studying different places or different time periods? What is the relative significance of each individual case study, in terms of the bigger picture?

Historians can apply theories or concepts to their case studies, or derive theories or concepts from their evidence, in order to bridge this interpretative gap. Theories can offer us hypotheses to test and then adopt or discard. Theories can also provide analytical tools or philosophical insights, which might help us to discern broader patterns in our case studies and understand how they relate to other examples. However, even with the benefit of theory, historians still often find it difficult to agree on what the bigger picture looks like. The problems are particularly marked for imperial historians, as the British empire was enormous, varied, and relatively long-lived. The British empire was not assembled according to a simple, state-sanctioned blueprint. It developed over a period of centuries, through the interaction of African, Asian, and other non-European societies with a motley assortment of British and non-British agents: missionaries, traders, soldiers, investors, settlers, miners, planters, and administrators, to name but a few. These interactions produced very different outcomes in different parts of the world. The overarching conceptual structures that might allow us to advance convincing answers to big questions thus seldom seem applicable to every part of the British empire, or across the broad sweep of the empire's long history. No single theory seems to offer a universal key for understanding every aspect of the history of the British empire, for answering each one of the fundamental questions which imperial historians together seek to address. Scholars have thus deployed a bewildering variety of theories and concepts to explain different aspects of the history of the British empire. Even then, each of these theories or concepts has attracted its critics as well as its champions, generating further unresolved debate.

Because of this, thinking about theory and the history of the British empire offers a particularly useful way of approaching the role of theory in the discipline of history more generally. Indeed, historians of the British empire have been inspired by (or have sought to discredit) many of the major theoretical innovations of recent times. As a result, the writing of British imperial history has been profoundly shaped by the wider theoretical waves that have swept, one after another, through the discipline of history. Thinking about the history of the British empire thus provides an excellent point of entry into what can otherwise be the abstract business of studying different approaches to and traditions of writing about the past.

Early histories of the British empire tended to be more-or-less uncritical, indeed often celebratory treatments of their subject. Their aim was as much to strengthen the British empire as to offer a dispassionate historical analysis of its origins and nature.[1] At the beginning of the twentieth century, a more oppositional set of accounts were written, highly polemical in tone, offering the first really coherent theories of imperial expansion. These typically adopted a Radical Liberal or Marxist perspective, as will be discussed in Chapter 1. Marxist-inspired histories continued to offer a significant take on empire into the 1980s at least. More recently, as Chapter 5 argues, global historians are now revisiting many of the issues that once exercised Marxist scholars.

During the 1950s, historians of what we might call 'high policy-making' began to engage seriously with the history of the modern British empire for the first time. In particular, the work of Ronald Robinson and John Gallagher established a tradition that is still alive today, dedicated to teasing out the economic, political, and strategic interests that shaped the nature of British imperial expansion, contraction, and rule. The focus in this literature is very much on the reasons, whether acknowledged by contemporaries or not, why policy-makers made the decisions that they did. It seeks the causes of imperial advance and retreat in the thought and actions of those at the pinnacle of British government. However, at the very same time that this new literature was emerging, the British empire was itself breaking up. **Decolonization** brought into being a whole range of successor states, intent on cementing their national independence and unity. It also produced a Britain shorn of its overseas accoutrements, and increasingly internally divided. Britain no longer seemed as formidable as it had been, its empire a thing of the past and thus not something of pressing contemporary concern. For many historians, the urgent task for their profession was now to write 'national histories', usable pasts that could help explain the origins and nature of the modern states that had been built on the ruins of empire. Sometimes these national histories were avowedly nationalist, seeking to underpin and strengthen the fragile new national identities that had emerged out of the colonial period. In such histories, the British empire was only trundled to centre-stage when a pantomime villain was needed: empire was the external force that had violated existing local cultures and political systems, destroying or suppressing the nation until nationalists had finally succeeded in driving the enemy back into the wings. In such accounts, there seemed little need to understand the British empire as a functioning world-system in and of itself, as a viable, coherent, and relatively long-lived whole.[2]

Perhaps due to this process of scholarly fragmentation and marginalization, imperial history was slow to engage with the shift towards social history that, from the 1960s onwards, shaped so many other branches of the discipline of history. Raphael Samuel defined social history as the history of 'ordinary' people, a history that engaged with contemporary social issues and had a clear social purpose.[3] During the 1970s and 1980s, some historians did seek to write about ordinary people and empire in this way.[4] The most sustained engagement with the social history agenda came from John MacKenzie, who pioneered the study of popular imperialism. MacKenzie's *Studies in Imperialism* series, published by Manchester University Press, became an important stimulus to and outlet for further research in this field.[5] An echo of E. P. Thompson's call to write 'history from below' (a history of those who had left little trace in the historical record and whose voices were thus seldom heard in conventional narratives) also sounded in Indian history, with the emergence of the Subaltern Studies school.[6]

Most recently, the writing of imperial history has been significantly reoriented by a wave of exciting new research. Since the 1990s, many historians of empire have followed the 'cultural turn' that, in the wake of the shift to writing social history, has reshaped the discipline of history more generally. The history of imperial policy-making has in the eyes of some scholars become unfashionable, and the economic history of empire even more so. Many have preferred instead to write about the cultural origins and consequences of empire. Some have called this the **new imperial history**, echoing the broader 'new cultural history', which had similar roots in a wide and eclectic body of cultural, literary, and anthropological theory, and which similarly focused on attitudes, assumptions, mentalities, and feelings, rather than on the ideas or systems of thought that had long been the familiar domain of intellectual historians. The **new imperial history** is in fact probably too diverse in its theoretical inspirations and conceptual preoccupations to be considered the product of a single school of historians, or to be defined too exactly. Nevertheless, some shared concerns and beliefs have surfaced again and again in this body of work.

First, much recent scholarship has been concerned with understanding how divisions of race, class, and gender influenced (and were influenced by) structures of dominance, hierarchy, and inequality in the British empire. Second, this recent work is often at pains to emphasize that Britain's own cultural development was shaped by empire, that Britain and its colonies were 'mutually constituted'. This latter point was picked up from Edward Said's influential study, *Orientalism* (1978): the **new imperial history** was in part inspired by the work of Said and other theorists of **postcolonialism**, but has also questioned or refined some of their claims.[7] Third, the **new imperial history** has sought to give more weight to 'non-elite and non-western pasts', reflecting the agenda and lasting influence of the Subaltern Studies school of South Asian history.[8] Whether the **new imperial history** has yet succeeded in this latter element of its quest is debateable. The desire to show how Britain's own history was shaped by empire has contributed to a much more outward-looking version of British history. Yet, for all its emphasis on racial inequalities and hierarchies, recent scholarship has also encouraged the writing of an imperial history that can seem overly preoccupied with the opinions, identities, and affairs of white people 'at home' in Britain.

After the cultural turn, many imperial historians now seem to be taking a 'global turn'. The history of the British empire is increasingly seen as central to the history of **globalization**, the creation of a more densely interconnected world order. This seemingly new historiographical growth in fact has deep roots. Marxists have long suggested that the role of the British empire was to usher in a modern, capitalist world economy. Robinson and Gallagher were not Marxists, but they too presented Britain's imperial history as part of its broader economic and strategic engagement with the wider world. And much of the **new imperial history** has been concerned to view Britain and its colonies in a global perspective, drawing on new departures in global and **transnational history**, and showing how complex, globe-spanning networks and reciprocal flows of influence linked together and shaped Britain and the disparate parts of the British empire.

► Definitions and concepts

Before we can navigate our way through the dense thicket of theories and concepts that has grown out of these changing approaches to imperial history, we first need to think about some of the key terms that we will encounter. The meanings of many of these terms are multiple and contested. Different historians can mean different things when they use words like 'empire', 'colony', 'imperialism', and 'colonialism'. Contemporaries also used them in a variety of ways, and sometimes in a fashion that virtually nobody would today. And often these labels have been applied with a frustrating lack of precision, even by those who have thought long and hard about the subject. As Lord Milner reflected in 1917, 'words like "Empire" hampered me certainly at every turn, though I have not the linguistic ability to get over it'.[9] Milner's career involved appointments as British High Commissioner in South Africa and British Colonial Secretary: if he could not define 'empire', then we should certainly pause for thought before we decide that we know what such words mean. We should be particularly wary of assuming that our own, contemporary understandings were shared by people in the past. As J. C. D. Clark notes, 'The use of anachronistic categories merely creates a world of shadows and fictions in which no clear questions can be asked and no clear answers can be given.'[10]

Although its classical and medieval origins are complex, in the modern period empire has generally come to mean 'rule over extensive, far-flung territories, far beyond the original "homeland" of the rulers'. Empires bring together a **periphery** of different territories, ethnicities, and religious and cultural groups, and put that periphery into some sort of unequal relationship with a dominant **core** territory (sometimes called the **metropole**) and its peoples.[11] However, even this common-sense definition raises questions. Some historians argue that 'rule' is not necessary for 'empire', that there exists a category of **informal empire** in which supposedly independent territories are so thoroughly dominated in economic terms that they enjoy little real sovereignty. They thus effectively become part of the **periphery**. As will be discussed in Chapter 1, some historians have seen China and parts of Latin America as the prime candidates to be considered for membership of Britain's nineteenth-century **informal empire**. Meanwhile, as we will see in Chapter 5, others have questioned whether terms like **core** and **periphery** are really helpful at all.

Britain's empire was composed of territories that we now often refer to using the blanket label 'colonies'. Yet this word begs questions too. In the past, people frequently used the term 'colony' to refer to a specific type of place, to which white British settlers had migrated to live permanently, in the process dispossessing or exterminating earlier inhabitants. This was 'colonization', on the model of ancient Greek settlement overseas. However, the word 'colony' has also been used by contemporaries and historians to describe places where small, temporarily resident groups of white officials presided over the government of large, non-white populations, places where little or no permanent British settlement took place: this was the ancient Roman model of empire. As early as 1849, the theorist Edward Gibbon Wakefield lamented this terminological slippage, claiming that the words 'colony' and 'colonization' were being 'used without a definite meaning, and even with different meanings'. Wakefield argued for greater precision, claiming that 'emigration and the permanent settlement of the emigrants on unoccupied land' were the key features of colonization. According to Wakefield, India was thus only a 'dependency', while Mauritius (which had been seized by Britain from France, and contained many French settlers) was 'a colony of France, but ... only a dependency of England', and the USA was still (despite its constitutional independence) best described as a colony of Britain.[12]

Wakefield clearly lost this rear-guard action. The historian Jürgen Osterhammel provides a useful working definition of what most scholars now understand the word 'colony' to mean: 'a new political organization created by invasion (conquest and/or settlement colonization) but built on pre-colonial conditions. Its alien rulers are in sustained dependence on a geographically remote "mother country" or imperial center, which claims exclusive rights of "possession" of the colony.'[13]

Similarly, despite Wakefield's protests, the meaning of the word 'colonization' has also changed over time. Today, historians seldom use the terms 'colonization' and 'white settlement' as synonyms. They now predominantly refer to the invasion and annexation of territory, and the subjugation and attempted cultural transformation of the inhabitants of annexed territory, as 'colonization', regardless of whether permanent white settlement was involved.

The meanings of the word 'imperialism' are particularly complex. In its broad sense, the term is often used today to describe general aggression against and sustained political, economic, or cultural domination over other countries. Yet it has also been used in much more specific ways: indeed, the historians Koebner and Schmidt claimed that the term changed its meaning no less than 12 times between the 1840s and the 1960s. Its original meaning in English, they argued, emerged during the 1840s and 1850s as contemporaries sought to describe France's Bonapartist style of government, and particularly the political methods of Louis Napoleon, who became Emperor Napoleon III of France in 1852 in the wake of a successful coup.

Napoleon III bought allegiance to the monarchy by impressing the people with the semblance of growing wealth at home and success abroad. He developed military prestige, let the army outshine civilian honours, and endeavoured to make the French a docile people basking in the imagination of national glory. This system of sentimental bondage was stigmatized as 'Imperialism'.[14]

Notably, Karl Marx claimed that Napoleon III had harnessed the 'imperialism of the peasant class' ('*den Imperialismus der Bauernklasse*') through state spectacle and appeals to patriotic sentiment.[15] According to Koebner and Schmidt, the word 'imperialism' only began to be applied to British policy in the 1870s, initially as a criticism of the showy and shallow adventurism of the British Prime Minister Benjamin Disraeli. The sense that 'imperialism' meant militarism, aggressive nationalism, and popular 'sentimental bondage' endured in subsequent decades, and became particularly prominent in the writings of Marxist and Radical Liberal commentators in the years before the First World War, as we will see in Chapter 1. It has never quite lost these resonances.

Today historians do not use the word 'imperialism' as much as they used to. This is partly due to an awareness of the awkward legacies of meaning inherited from previous generations, and partly because of the widespread post-1989 academic shift away from overtly Marxist modes of analysis.[16] Instead, many scholars now write about 'colonialism'. However, the meaning of this word is not immediately obvious: it has become, like 'colony' and 'colonization', a catch-all term used to describe a wide range of phenomena, processes, and inequalities. Its meaning has also been heavily influenced by the emergence of **postcolonialism** and associated new approaches to the imperial past. Historians who use the word 'colonialism' tend to emphasize the pervasive, systematic, and transformative nature of imperial influence over all aspects of a colony's economy, politics, society, and culture, and indeed over the metropolitan power itself. They also stress the role of perceived and purposely constructed racial differences and hierarchies in separating rulers from ruled, and in facilitating all forms of exploitation of the latter on the grounds of their supposed inferiority. Again, Osterhammel has provided a useful description of how the word is now generally used:

Colonialism is a relationship of domination between an indigenous (or forcibly imported) majority and a minority of foreign invaders. The fundamental decisions affecting the lives of the colonized people are made and implemented by the colonial rulers in pursuit of interests that are often defined in a distant metropolis. Rejecting cultural compromises with the colonized population, the colonizers are convinced of their own superiority and of their ordained mandate to rule.[17]

However, as will be seen throughout the chapters that follow, some historians have questioned whether the varied and complex histories of the diverse relationships and structures that constituted the British empire can meaningfully be evoked by a single word. This reflects a more fundamental divide between those who think that the British empire was (and, indeed, that empires in general were) driven by one big ideological 'project' of 'colonialism', and those who argue that the British empire involved so many different impulses that it cannot be analysed as a single, unified enterprise.

All this uncertainty is frustrating. Yet we can use it as a stimulus to sharpen our own thinking. It is worth striving to understand what contemporaries meant when they used different words, what historians have meant, and what we ourselves mean when we use them. For such terms are the basic building blocks for the more ambitious conceptual and theoretical structures that have been developed to make sense of the imperial past. If we do not form those blocks carefully, then the larger structures can bear little analytical weight. Words are also valuable indicators of the underlying political beliefs or ideologies that have shaped the ways that people have thought, and continue to think, about empire. Whether historians choose, consciously or otherwise, to write of 'imperialism', 'colonialism', or 'overseas expansion' can be extremely significant, for each term is freighted with a range of political and other meanings. We might be tempted to reject words like 'imperialism' and 'colonialism' entirely, as too vague and imprecise, but if we do so then our accounts of the past risk becoming 'etiolated and bloodless ... little more than a litany of special cases or an elegy of exceptions ... [ignoring] the ruthless drive for dominance in the overseas world which periodically seized metropolitan statesmen, missionaries, soldiers, and sailors'.[18] Words like 'imperialism' and 'colonialism' remind us that the history of the British empire is a history of violence.

▶ Processes and places

As noted earlier, the concepts and theories used by imperial historians have generally emerged out of, or been discussed in the context of, more specific analyses of particular places and periods. These theories and concepts often bear the marks of the specific case studies that they were applied to or devised to explain. In the chapters that follow, it will become clear that, frequently, they cannot be extended in any straightforward fashion to a broader set of

historical examples. Yet in their debates about the usefulness of different concepts and theories, imperial historians sometimes seem unaware that they are
not comparing like with like. The remainder of this introduction offers a very
brief outline of the history of the British empire, to help contextualize the specific case studies from which different theories and concepts have been drawn.

Some historians trace the roots of British overseas expansion to deep-
seated processes of 'internal colonialism', generated by the aggressive expansion of the English state into surrounding Welsh, Scottish, and Irish territory.
Although originating in the medieval period, these processes were hardly complete by the eighteenth century, as continued unrest and rebellion in Scotland
and Ireland indicated. To many the status of Ireland remained ambiguous
until independence in 1921, and beyond: in some ways Ireland was a colony
of Britain (or England), and yet also a constituent part of the imperial core.[19]
Nevertheless, during the nineteenth century the integration of England, Wales,
Scotland, and Ireland into the United Kingdom was supported by the forging
of an overarching British identity. The overseas counterpart of this was the
construction of a self-consciously British empire, channelling the efforts of the
four nations into a common endeavour.

By the mid-eighteenth century the key support areas of British overseas wealth
and power lay in the Caribbean and along the east coast of North America. As
will be discussed in Chapter 5, according to the historian Kenneth Pomeranz,
the exploitation of the resources of these areas provided the basis for the subsequent, dramatic growth of the British economy. Historians have also seen this
empire as an important part of a wider 'Atlantic World', binding the European
and American continents together.[20] This was an empire of white settlement, by
people who claimed to retain the rights and liberties of 'free-born Englishmen'. It
was also an empire based on black slavery, and on a rigorous system of commercial regulation and management known as mercantilism. For Britain the most
valuable territories, in terms of wealth generated and commodities available for
export, lay in the island colonies of the West Indies. Here, British control dated
back to the early seventeenth century. Large-scale sugar plantations were worked
by African slaves and supported the prosperous white planter elite. An estimated
930,000 slaves were transported by the British in the period 1761–1808, at a
cost of enormous dislocation, suffering, and loss of life.[21] As will be discussed in
Chapter 3, social and cultural histories of the slave colonies of the West Indies
have formed the basis for attempts by many historians of race and gender to
explain the underpinnings and consequences of British imperial expansion.

The American Revolution partially destroyed this 'First British Empire', or at
least led to a drastic reconstruction of the geographical and ideological foundations of British power overseas. Even before the loss of the Thirteen Colonies ·
on the North American mainland, Britain had been engaged in carving out

a vast new territorial empire in South Asia. The resulting 'swing to the east' saw what to some amounted to the founding of a 'Second British Empire'.[22] British commercial interests in India had long been extended and safeguarded by the British East India Company, a private trading concern that had been granted a profitable monopoly over British trade with the Far East in order to encourage British merchants to engage in this risky business. During the eighteenth century, the Company became increasingly militarized, as it sought to defend and advance its commercial interests in an unstable political environment. A turning point came when the failing Mughal emperor granted the Company administrative responsibility for the whole province of Bengal, including 20 million people and control of the associated tax revenues from land. 'Company rule' began in earnest, with Bengal providing the launch pad for further British territorial expansion. This was a strange type of empire: a private company (only supported and regulated by the British government in a loose fashion) trading, administering territory, taxing peasants, and controlling large armies composed predominantly of Indian soldiers (**sepoys**). But it was empire nonetheless, and lasted until the British crown finally took control of the *raj* in the wake of the Indian Mutiny and Rising of 1857–1858.

The historiography of Britain's empire in India is rich and complex, and has generated some of the key theories and concepts that imperial historians have subsequently sought to apply more widely. As will be discussed in Chapter 1, for historians such as Christopher Bayly, any explanation of the nature and causes of British imperial expansion must be centrally concerned with India. Historians of colonial rule have used Indian examples to develop and contest theories about 'colonial knowledge', examined in Chapter 2. What has become known as the 'Cambridge school' of historians has meanwhile used the history of Indian engagement with and resistance to British imperial authority as a means to develop the concept of **collaboration**, and to challenge simplistic assumptions about the existence of an inevitable antagonism between the forces of nationalism and imperialism. We will examine these ideas in greater depth in Chapters 3 and 4.

During the French Revolutionary and Napoleonic Wars (1793–1815), British policy-makers protected the routes to their now-crucial support area in India by occupying and annexing a chain of territories, including the Cape Colony in southern Africa and Ceylon off the southern tip of the Indian peninsula. Further east, British penal colonies in New South Wales, Van Diemen's Land (Tasmania), and Norfolk Island limped along as commercially and strategically marginal dumping grounds for convicts transported from Britain and Ireland. As a new sheep-rearing economy developed, more free settlers came to New South Wales, generating significant levels of frontier violence as whites dispossessed Aborigines of their land and turned it over to pasturage. Over the following decades, white settlement would continue in southern Africa, Australia, the remaining British North American colonies (modern-day Canada), and later in New Zealand. By the late nineteenth century these places had become central to Britain's world-system. To protect its commercial interests, Britain also maintained a system of island outposts in the Mediterranean and elsewhere. Over the course of the nineteenth century, policy-makers meanwhile continued to safeguard the commercial and strategic interests of the Indian *raj* through the acquisition of Singapore and Malacca (brought together with Penang to form the Straits Settlements in 1826), agreements with the Malay States, territorial expansion into Burma, and the opening up of the Chinese market to British commerce through gun-boat diplomacy and the establishment of treaty ports.[23] As already mentioned, analysis of the economic influence exerted over China by Britain in this period, and over parts of Latin America, forms the basis for the concept of **informal empire**, discussed in Chapter 1.

Particularly from the 1830s onwards, the British empire was transformed by a wave of changes, some of which reflected new ways of thinking among the British governing elite: the end of the slave trade (1807) was followed by the abolition of slavery (1834); the old mercantilist system of commercial regulation was replaced by the ideology and policies of free trade; and 'responsible self-government' was extended to white settler assemblies. However, the effects of this transformation were not felt evenly across the empire. In India, neither demilitarization nor democratization made much progress. In the West Indies, the abolition of slavery gave many blacks greater control over their lives, but free trade proved a disaster, exposing sugar producers to cheap foreign competition (some of it dependent on slave labour) and subjecting the islands to decades of economic decline.

It was in the so-called white settler colonies that the transition to a 'liberal' empire seemed most real. From the mid-nineteenth century onwards, many of the settler colonies experienced dramatic levels of economic growth. This was accompanied and facilitated by unprecedented settler demographic expansion, fuelled by migration from Britain and Ireland and driving an export-led cycle of boom-and-bust development, swamping indigenous populations in the process. 'Explosive colonisation' created large communities of settlers who claimed to be British, and who were closely tied to Britain by economic interest, cultural affinity, and demands for military protection against internal and external challenges.[24] Recently, historians have devoted a great deal of attention to examining the nature of this settler diaspora and its relationship with Britain, and have developed the idea of the 'British world' as a means to understand it, as will be discussed in Chapter 4.

In Africa before 1880, Britain and the other European powers generally limited themselves to occupying small colonial enclaves in coastal regions. It was hoped, often in vain, that these outposts would be sufficient to open up the interior of the continent to trade with Europe. Only in Egypt and in southern Africa were British economic interests substantial, and only in the latter region did Britain establish extensive formal colonies, at the Cape and in Natal. However, this situation was radically transformed by the events of the last two decades of the nineteenth century, when the Scramble for Africa (also known as the Partition of Africa) took place. In a short space of time, Britain and a number of other European powers staked formal claims to govern huge new expanses of African territory, together encompassing almost the entire continent. Britain occupied Egypt in 1882, and over the following two decades established protectorates over British East Africa (Kenya), Uganda, and British Central Africa (Nyasaland) and extended existing colonial enclaves in Sierra Leone, Gold Coast, and Nigeria. Settler colonies in southern Africa also expanded and were held (using force where necessary) within Britain's orbit. Since the beginning of the twentieth century, some of the classic theories purporting to explain the causes and course of British imperial expansion have derived from analysis of the Scramble, as we will see in Chapter 1. Research on colonial rule in Africa has also questioned and complicated theories about the nature of the colonial state, discussed in Chapter 2. Expansion in the Pacific (Fiji was annexed in 1874, and British New Guinea was made a protectorate in 1884) has also been examined by historians in the context of the 'new imperialism' of the late nineteenth century.

The twentieth-century history of the British empire cannot be explained in terms of a simple process of decline and fall.[25] The ramshackle global system of power and influence inherited from the Victorians survived the First World War, and in some ways seemed more unified than ever before, capable of transforming itself in the interwar years into a 'Third British Empire' that successfully contained the challenge of white settler and Indian demands for increased autonomy.[26] As we will see in Chapter 4, it is misleading to present the British empire as collapsing in the face of an implacable nationalist opposition: the politics of identity in the interwar empire were far more complicated than this. **Communalism**, the fierce antagonisms that divided different ethnic, linguistic, and religious groups, proved a powerful force, challenging imperial policy-makers and nationalist leaders alike in India, and bringing civil unrest and repression to Britain's interwar 'Mandate' in Palestine (effectively a colony). As discussed in Chapter 1, historians of **decolonization** have devoted considerable attention to the subsequent strains placed on Britain's world-system by the Second World War and its aftermath. They have examined the shifting perspectives of policy-makers who sought to gauge Britain's economic and strategic requirements overseas, and to measure the costs and benefits of a continued formal imperial presence.

The main chapters of this book draw on a wide range of writings about the history of the British empire, focusing on the nineteenth and twentieth centuries and incorporating relevant work concerning many different places. The history of the seventeenth- and eighteenth-century British empire is not treated in depth here, reflecting the fact that it has developed historiographical traditions of its own, involving a somewhat different set of concepts and theories.[27]

The book has been organized so as to bring out the key questions that imperial historians have asked, and the concepts and theories that they have developed in attempting to provide answers to them. The structure of the book also seeks to illustrate how broader approaches to writing history – political, economic, social, and cultural – have influenced historians studying the British empire, and to demonstrate the affinities as well as the tensions between different approaches to understanding the imperial past. Chapter 1 considers the 'why' and 'how' of British imperial expansion. Why did Britain establish and expand its empire? How were the decisions made that led to the annexation of new territory? Subsequent chapters are also concerned with the 'how' of expansion, but broaden out the scope of analysis considerably. Chapter 2 examines the political structures harnessed or established by the British to run their empire. Chapters 3 and 4 discuss the social and cultural frameworks which supported colonial rule. All of these chapters consider the consequences of empire: how it re-shaped social structures, but also how it often failed to transform pre-colonial patterns totally; the ways that empire conditioned experiences and perceptions of difference, but also the role of empire as a force for social and cultural integration; the ways that empire encouraged people to think about themselves and others, and to identify with wider communities. Chapter 5 brings all these issues together in the context of the recent global turn in scholarship. It looks at how historians have tried to write empire into emerging global histories that narrate and explain the development of the increasingly interconnected world of which we are today so aware. Clearly, debates about the big questions in British imperial history are not over yet.

1 Expansion and Contraction

▶ The 'why' and 'how' of empire-building

Why did the British establish and expand their empire? It is possible to answer this question in a number of ways. A basic, pseudo-psychological approach has some instinctive appeal: we might assume that empire was the direct result of a simple thirst for power, an innate human drive that has influenced societies and people throughout history. British empire-building could be seen as one notable example of how this impulse could take hold of a nation. Yet it would be hard to verify such a claim using any historical method of enquiry: there is no accepted apparatus for understanding mass psychology. Moreover, such a simplistic theory could not explain why it was the *British* empire that came to enjoy such predominance over European and non-European rivals during the late eighteenth and nineteenth centuries, unless we accept the facile claim that the British are a uniquely power-hungry and belligerent people.

Such a basic explanation would also leave us in the dark as to the 'how' of imperial expansion: the thinking behind territorial annexations and the reasons advanced by contemporaries to explain the decisions they made; the interaction of different British historical actors with each other and with a wide range of non-British agents; and the role of broader economic, social, and cultural forces (and not forgetting chance and contingency) in shaping the 'successes' and 'failures' of British imperial expansion. Any attempt to explain the sudden contraction of the British empire after the Second World War in terms of a general 'loss of nerve', a sapping of the will to power, is bound to leave us in a similarly benighted state.

Some have argued that economic theories provide the best basis for understanding imperial expansion. In the early twentieth century, Radical Liberals in Britain and Marxists in Continental Europe argued that imperial policy was determined by the commercial and financial requirements of various interest groups which all had something to gain from overseas expansion. This way of thinking about the 'why' of empire left an enduring imprint on historical scholarship, partly because of the wide diffusion of Marxist thought through the discipline of history during the twentieth century, and partly because of a lack of empirical research that could verify or disprove such theories. It was only during the 1950s that historians began systematically to examine the archival record relating to imperial policy-making in late nineteenth-century Britain. From this point onwards the availability of fresh evidence combined with a distrust of 'vulgar' Marxist explanations of historical change to produce a new body of historical writing about the British empire. Rather than emphasize economic forces, much of this literature focused on political processes. Instead of seeking out the influence of hidden commercial or financial interest groups, it examined the reasoning behind the decisions made by politicians and civil servants, the workings of the so-called **official mind**.

This chapter examines the 'classic' Marxist and Radical Liberal theories of imperialism, before discussing the very different approach adopted by historians of 'high policy-making'. The chapter then surveys the work of P. J. Cain and A. G. Hopkins, who have sought to return economic forces to the centre of discussions of the 'why' and 'how' of British imperialism. An understanding of the economic relationships and material forces shaping patterns of British overseas engagement is clearly essential if we want to have a full picture of British imperial expansion and contraction. Yet, as the Austrian economist and political scientist Joseph Schumpeter noted in the early twentieth century (partly in response to Marxist theories), we should not seek to explain empire in terms of a single motivating force, economic or otherwise. Alongside 'official' reasons, such as the desire to spread a particular religion or model of 'civilization', always lay a mixture of other, often unacknowledged motives for empire: 'lust for blood and booty, avarice and the craving for power, sexual impulses, commercial interests... [and] instincts to which a warlike past has given predominance in the mentality'. Indeed, as Schumpeter hinted, we might not be able to explain empire purely or even primarily in terms of rational interests or decision-making processes.[1] Many historians have thus preferred to adopt pluralist explanations of imperial expansion and contraction. According to this perspective, the complex interactions of a wide range of forces and agents together worked to set the agenda for policy-makers and shaped the outcome of their decisions.

Reflecting the focus of the historiography, much of the discussion in this chapter turns on the so-called new imperialism of the 1880s and 1890s, and particularly the Scramble for Africa. The chapter also considers late eighteenth-century expansion in South Asia, which has similarly acted as a key case study for historians seeking to understand the growth of the British empire. Our understanding of the 'why' and 'how' of British imperial contraction – **decolonization** – is less well-developed. This is partly because the history of twentieth-century British **decolonization** has been less thoroughly 'theorized' than the history of nineteenth-century British expansion.[2] It is also because state archives have only been made available relatively recently and because, as we are now discovering, the British state may in fact have purposely hidden a significant body of evidence from the scrutiny of historians.

▶ Capitalists, financiers, and imperialism

In 1902 the Radical Liberal journalist and economist J. A. Hobson published *Imperialism: A Study*. While the contemporary impact of his book was limited, Hobson's theories proved highly influential in shaping how subsequent generations of scholars approached the history of the British empire.

To comprehend Hobson's theories, it is first necessary to understand what he meant by 'imperialism'. Hobson drew a fundamental distinction between what he saw as legitimate and illegitimate forms of territorial expansion. In Canada, Australia, and New Zealand, what he called 'colonialism' – which he defined as the permanent settlement of British migrants overseas – had represented 'a natural overflow of nationality'. British migrants had occupied 'vacant or sparsely peopled foreign lands' in order to establish free and self-governing communities. This represented 'a territorial enlargement of the stock, language and institutions of the nation', spreading democratic British values. All this, Hobson thought, had been legitimate, even desirable. It was not 'imperialism'. Hobson did not remark on the violence and dispossession that white settlement had meant for the previous inhabitants of such places.

So what, for Hobson, was 'imperialism'? In 1902, when he published his book, Britain was engaged in the final stages of a bloody war in South Africa to crush the autonomy of the Boers, white settlers of predominantly Dutch descent. This war, Hobson argued, was the product of a 'spurious' form of 'colonialism', very different from expansion in Canada and Australasia. He predicted that in South Africa the desire to exercise autocratic rule over the vanquished Boers, and over large numbers of black Africans, would prevent any attempt to implant British 'civilization'. Democratic values would not be applied to South Africa. Hobson identified the same basic problem with much of Britain's territorial expansion since the early 1880s. In Britain's newer tropical colonies in Africa, Asia, and the Pacific there seemed to be no prospect of extending self-government to colonial subjects. A white minority would rule despotically for the foreseeable future. The fact that a range of other European powers, and the US, were now constructing similarly authoritarian tropical empires made the situation even more troubling. The world was no longer heading towards a bright future of internationalism, of unrestricted and peaceful interaction between nation-states (as free traders had long hoped), but into a nightmare scenario of great power rivalry, empire-building, militarism, aggression, and war. As autocracy spread in the colonies, so liberty would be undermined at home, with empire-building distracting parliament and people from domestic inequalities, encouraging irrational and aggressive nationalism, and entrenching the power of selfish interest groups and the military.[3]

For Hobson, this was 'imperialism' or the 'new imperialism' (Hobson used the two terms more-or-less interchangeably): aggressive European rivalries, driven by the desire to control tropical colonies, and mobilizing the masses behind foreign policies from which most people realized few material benefits.

Where did the motives for this new imperialism spring from? According to Hobson, the drive to territorial expansion did not reflect national economic interests. Tropical colonies generated very little trade, and made no significant overall contribution to Britain's national wealth. At the same time, participation in imperial rivalries saddled the British taxpayer with a massively increased bill for military expenditure. Thus, Hobson argued, the motives for the new imperialism had to derive from the selfish requirements of certain 'economic parasites': 'the business interests of the nation as a whole are subordinated to those of certain sectional interests that usurp control of the national resources and use them for their private gain'.[4]

Hobson argued that during the late nineteenth century, industrial enterprises had used new and more productive machines and worked on a larger and more efficient scale, increasing output while keeping wages low. They had thus begun to produce much more than could be consumed at home. Wealth had not been distributed evenly or fairly. Workers were too poor to purchase the fruits of the modern industrial economy, while industrialists amassed fortunes larger than they could ever spend (in the US, this process had been exacerbated by the creation of monopolies or trusts). Hobson argued that the savings of the wealthy represented 'surplus capital' that had to be re-invested because it could not be spent. Returns on investments at home had dwindled in a congested, overproducing domestic economy, so surplus capital was exported overseas. Imperialism was in turn driven by the desire of investors to secure and protect areas into which they could plough their surplus capital.

In Britain and in other imperial nations, Hobson argued, investors had bent the state to their will in order to secure profitable colonial outlets for surplus capital.

> It is not too much to say that the modern foreign policy of Great Britain has been primarily a struggle for profitable markets of investment. To a larger extent every year Great Britain has been becoming a nation living upon tribute from abroad, and the classes who enjoy this tribute have had an ever-increasing incentive to employ the public policy, the public purse, and the public force

to extend the field of their private investments, and to safeguard and improve their existing investments.

A range of other parasites had also benefited from the process of imperial expansion: armaments manufacturers; shipbuilders; producers of certain export goods; aristocrats and others seeking profitable postings overseas; and (most significantly for Hobson) the financiers who channelled surplus capital to the colonies. Financiers manipulated markets, governments, and popular patriotism in order to maximize their gains and those of their clients. Hobson's arguments were shaped by a significant element of anti-Semitism: many working in the world of finance were 'men of a single and peculiar race' – Jews – who he claimed were particularly willing to manipulate the policies of the different nations for their own profit. Hobson's arguments were also influenced by a powerful Radical Liberal desire for social reform. The best way to eliminate imperialism, Hobson argued, was to redistribute income so that workers could afford to consume what industry produced, thus preventing the accumulation of surplus capital.[5]

In the decade that followed, Continental European Marxist thinkers presented similar ideas about the origins of imperialism. Some drew directly on Hobson's writings. One of the first coherent Marxist theories of imperialism was formulated by the Austrian Marxist Rudolf Hilferding, in his book *Das Finanzkapital* (published in 1910). Hilferding argued that industry was increasingly organizing itself into monopolies, forming links with large banks and financial institutions, and lobbying for tariff protection, all in order to maintain prices and profits. Imperialism was the export version of this monopolistic urge, the quest to control supplies of raw materials, labour, and markets beyond the nation's borders, achieved by subordinating the state to the needs of capital. Yet Hilferding was not primarily thinking of British colonial expansion when he wrote of imperialism. He was more interested in understanding the nature of German and Austrian 'finance capitalism', the aggressive policies these countries adopted towards their neighbours, and the consequences for socialist politics of industrial concentration, tariff protection, and militarism. Imperialism meant economic rivalries between the European powers. Hilferding believed that these antagonisms would eventually inevitably boil over into war and the final collapse of capitalism. He sought to predict the European future rather than to understand the colonial past.

Other European Marxist critics adopted a similar line of analysis. In *Die Akkumulation des Kapitals* (published in 1913), Rosa Luxemburg argued for a long-running capitalist history of violence that included colonial expansion. However, like Hilferding, she defined 'imperialism' primarily in terms of early twentieth-century monopolies, tariffs, and militarism. In 'Der Imperialismus', an article published a few weeks before the outbreak of the First World War, Karl Kautsky repeated many of the ideas formulated by Hilferding and Luxemburg, and drew on notions of underconsumption and surplus capital, but also pondered whether European capitalism might be able to adapt in order to delay its final crisis.[6]

V. I. Lenin offered a fierce rebuttal of this latter possibility in *Imperialism: the Highest Stage of Capitalism*, published in 1916 in the midst of the war. Lenin's study became the key Marxist work of reference for subsequent discussions of imperialism, although it constituted a synthesis of previous Marxist (and British Radical Liberal) thinking, rather than an entirely original contribution. Like other Marxist writers, Lenin equated 'imperialism' with early twentieth-century militarized economic rivalries between the European powers, fuelled by monopoly and finance capitalism. Powerful capitalist interests had, he argued, obliged the state to seek exclusive access to external markets, labour supplies, raw materials, and investment opportunities for surplus capital. Imperialism generated a whole range of aggressive foreign policies, not just colonial territorial expansion: it also encompassed, for example, the subordination of supposedly independent countries, a process by which they became 'semi-colonies'. For Lenin imperialism *was* capitalism, in its 'highest' – and therefore final – form. There was no possibility that it could reform itself out of its terminal crisis. The First World War was, he argued, a manifestation of this crisis, with the great powers fighting for control of the world's resources.[7]

For historians, theories are built on, applied to, and tested by case studies. Debate often revolves around whether a particular theory can be extended from one, possibly narrow, case study or group of case studies to a wider set of examples. In the case of Radical Liberal and Marxist theories of imperialism, it is important to understand the case studies upon which they were based, and to which their originators intended them to apply.

Hobson's book, published in 1902, claimed to explain the previous two decades of imperial expansionism. However, much of his argument was extrapolated from a more recent and narrow case study: Hobson's own, first-hand, observations of the crisis in South Africa that had preceded the war of 1899–1902. Hobson had travelled in the region just before the outbreak of the war, writing reports for the Liberal *Manchester Guardian* newspaper. He believed that it was the wealthy mining capitalists in South Africa who had pushed the British government to break the power of the Boers, in order to secure their own economic interests. Many of his more general claims about imperialism were inspired by this example. Hobson's book also contained some detailed discussion of recent Western involvement in China. Aside from this, his analysis rested on tables of figures about territorial expansion, trade, and investment, and on unverified claims about the supposed connections between those different sets of figures. Ultimately, he asserted that financial and industrial interests were what drove imperial expansion, but provided little in the way of conclusive proof that this was the case.[8] He did not offer any concrete evidence that financiers or other interest groups had pushed British policy-makers to expand, and he did not even try to examine in any detail the official thinking behind individual episodes of territorial annexation, in South Africa or elsewhere. As Peter Cain (an historian who is by no means unsympathetic to Hobson's approach) concludes: 'the questions he asked were of real interest to students of British imperialism, but ... the answers he offered sometimes did not fit the known facts very well'.[9] *Imperialism: A Study* was a work of contemporary comment rather than of historical analysis, and was meant to support several of Hobson's immediate, domestic political objectives. It was an appeal to members of the Liberal Imperialist faction (which had supported British policy in South Africa) to see the error of their ways and to reject aggressive diplomacy. The book also reflected his attempts to refocus the Liberal party's political programme on social reform.

Marxist theories of imperialism were meanwhile based on an entirely different set of case studies, which had little to do with the British empire at all. As already noted, Continental Marxists were not primarily interested in colonial empires, or in explaining late nineteenth-century European expansion in Africa and Asia. They were seeking to analyse the aggressive foreign, military, and economic policies of the central European states, especially Austria and Germany. Colonial empires were, for contemporary Marxist writers, far from the sole or even the defining element in European imperialism. Like Hobson, Continental Marxists were pursuing contemporary political agendas, writing with an eye on the present and seeking to shape the future. Paradoxically, Marxist theories of imperialism may be of more relevance to historians of Europe than to imperial historians.

Nevertheless, the writings of Hobson and his Marxist contemporaries inspired some subsequent writers to develop more general accounts of British empire-building and imperial rule, which presented economic considerations and the lobbying activities of commercial and financial interest groups as the prime motivators of expansion. Both Leonard Woolf, in his *Empire and Commerce in Africa: A Study in Economic Imperialism* (1919), and Parker Thomas Moon, in *Imperialism and World Politics* (1926), thus for example applied economic theories of empire more widely to British imperial history.[10]

However, other historians were deeply sceptical about this approach. W. K. Hancock was an early critic, famously claiming that 'Imperialism is no word for scholars'. Hancock meant that imperialism was too vague and polemical a term to have any real meaning as a category for historical analysis.[11] From the 1950s onwards, a new generation of imperial historians launched a devastating cumulative assault on the idea that overseas territorial expansion was driven by the needs of parasitic economic interests. They alleged that Hobson and his Marxist contemporaries had taken pre-conceived theoretical constructs and had merely asserted that they explained imperial expansion, without questioning whether the available evidence really supported their claims. David Fieldhouse argued that the writings of Hobson and Marxist critics amounted to 'an inductive theory whose theoretical basis existed long before those events which it was eventually used to explain'.[12] Ronald Robinson similarly claimed that Marxist theories of imperialism were 'deduced more from first principle than empirical observation'.[13]

▶ **Informal empire and the official mind**

In 1953 Ronald Robinson and John Gallagher published 'The Imperialism of Free Trade', and radically reoriented debates about economic interests and British overseas expansion. The article was a brilliant if necessarily short and impressionistic overview, seeking to overturn the established historical wisdom that Britain had moved from a mid-nineteenth-century policy of pacific free trade to an aggressive late nineteenth-century policy of imperial expansion. Robinson and Gallagher instead argued for an underlying continuity in Victorian policy-making. They claimed that statesmen and civil servants had worked throughout this period to secure the country's economic interests overseas, and had construed those interests in broad national terms. The state had not been the mere tool of individual companies or lobby groups, but rather an impartial arbiter of a diverse range of British interests. Robinson and Gallagher also argued that, in pursuing national economic interests, policy-makers had been able to pick from a range of tools as the occasion demanded, selecting the one best-suited for securing British overseas requirements at any given moment. **Formal empire** – the annexation of territory – had been merely one of several available options. 'Refusals to annex are no proof of reticence to control.'[14]

For Robinson and Gallagher, **formal empire** had to be understood in the context of the wider processes by which British economic involvement overseas had expanded during the nineteenth century, of Britain's overall engagement with global patterns of trade, production, and finance. As overseas economic expansion had continued on a broad front, the British state had extended its oversight to places where British subjects were sending migrants, goods, and money, and from which they were drawing raw materials and foodstuffs. In many cases, the British state merely observed, and did not intervene. British economic activity often went on without political intervention, without compromising the sovereignty of the country's trading partners. Although British trade with the United States and Europe was extensive, empire was never on the cards. Elsewhere, **informal empire** was required: British policy-makers exerted political influence, and perhaps intervened periodically with military force, in order to ensure that certain areas of the world furnished British enterprise with what it required. But they stopped short of wholesale annexation. China and Latin America were the key examples here. Finally, in some areas, **formal empire** was necessary. In parts of Asia, Africa, and the Pacific, the only way to secure Britain's economic or strategic requirements was to annex the relevant territories and govern their affairs directly. Formal annexation was thus a 'function of economic expansion', but not a 'necessary function': British economic involvement in a territory did not always make annexation necessary or even desirable.[15] For Robinson and Gallagher, free-trade treaties, gunboat diplomacy, and territorial annexation were all forms of what they called 'imperialism', and were all consequences of British economic expansion and of the global oversight exercised by the British state.

Thus, according to Robinson and Gallagher, it was wrong to divide up British imperial history into phases of eager eighteenth-century mercantilist empire-building, mid-nineteenth-century free-trading anti-imperialism, and aggressive late-Victorian 'new imperialism'. They emphasized that, across the whole period, statesmen were ready to protect British interests overseas by applying whatever form of pressure was deemed most effective in the circumstances, and willing to annex territory when it seemed absolutely necessary to do so. The mid-nineteenth century saw the extension of **formal empire** to key points in Africa, Asia, and the Pacific, and the strengthening of British informal influence in southern Africa, Latin America, and China. **Informal empire** had to be understood, Robinson and Gallagher argued, as just as significant a component of British imperialism as **formal empire**: 'Economic expansion in the mid-Victorian age was matched by a corresponding political expansion which has been overlooked because it could not be seen by that study of maps which, it has been said, drives sane men mad.'[16]

Robinson and Gallagher's analysis overlapped with that of Hobson and of Marxist writers in some significant ways. Their definition of 'imperialism' was similarly broad, extending beyond formal expansion, and their concept of **informal empire** chimed with Lenin's category of 'semi-colonial' territories. However, their analysis diverged from Marxist theories in key respects. Crucially, Robinson and Gallagher claimed that British policy-makers saw annexation as a last resort. They much preferred not to intervene, or to limit intervention to informal means wherever possible, because they wanted to avoid the expense and complications of formal colonial rule: the maxim of imperial policy was 'trade with informal control if possible; trade with rule when necessary'.[17] It followed from this that when the British presence in a region switched from **informal** to **formal empire**, this might reflect not the eager seizing of an opportunity, but instead the grudging acceptance of an unavoidable burden. Policy-makers might have been obliged to undertake formal annexation as a result of the economic turbulence generated by British involvement, but non-economic considerations sometimes also forced their hands. Dismissing earlier theories of imperialism, Robinson and Gallagher argued that it was unnecessary to seek out hidden economic interest groups that manipulated Britain into late nineteenth-century imperial expansion, or a crisis of capitalism that obliged policy-makers to annex territory to provide protected markets for British trade or investment. Instead, they emphasized the significance of contemporary thinking about British national economic, strategic, and geopolitical interests, which at certain times and in particular places obliged reluctant policy-makers to annex territory.

Crucially, Robinson and Gallagher also questioned **Eurocentric** economic theories of imperialism. They suggested that the decision to annex could be driven by events at the **periphery**, rather than by forces generated in the **metropole**. It was when existing social, economic, and state structures in the **periphery** proved too weak to deliver British requirements, creating a crisis that threatened British interests, that the shift from informal influence to **formal empire** became necessary. According to Robinson and Gallagher, in the 1880s British policy-makers only participated in the Scramble for Africa

> as a painful but unavoidable necessity which arose from a threat of foreign expansion and the irrepressible tendency of trade to overflow the bounds of empire [and from the] absence there of large-scale, strong, indigenous political organizations which had served informal expansion so well elsewhere.

Expansion in Africa was not a consequence of the lobbying of profit-seeking capitalists, but instead a reluctant extension of authority over territory of marginal economic importance, driven by the collapse of local state structures: 'in tropical Africa the imperialists were merely scraping the bottom of the barrel.'[18]

In 'The Imperialism of Free Trade', Robinson and Gallagher implied that British policy-makers were clear-sighted and rational, and that they shared a common set of assumptions and guiding principles. Policy-makers aimed to serve the nation's overall economic interests, and worked according to an objective measure of those interests. Robinson and Gallagher refined these assumptions in their subsequent book, *Africa and the Victorians*, which developed the concept of the **official mind**. Here they argued that in a strikingly homogenous political system, British statesmen and civil servants had worked together to assess available information and develop responses to policy challenges, guided by 'the long-run national interest which stayed much the same from ministry to ministry, regardless of the ideological stock in trade of the Party in power'. Policy-makers, they claimed, played a larger role than any other group in shaping the course of events. Crucially, policy-makers were generally able to pursue long-term national interests without favouring any one particular group: 'It was their high calling to mediate between jarring and selfish interests and to keep the state from being used as the tool of any of them.' As a result, for Robinson and Gallagher, examining the **official mind** of London-based policy-making offered the best way to understand empire-building. Indeed they suggested that in the Scramble for Africa, given a lack of any popular or commercial pressure for expansion, the **official mind** might have itself played a significant role in generating the forces leading to annexation.[19]

Yet, in contrast to 'The Imperialism of Free Trade', in *Africa and the Victorians* Robinson and Gallagher did not present a picture of cool-headed policy-makers devising policy along rational, perfectly informed lines. They did not suggest that policies were always clearly thought through, or that they always produced their intended outcomes. Personalities played a major role: 'the hopes, the memories and neuroses' of individual policy-makers had to be taken into account. Moreover, policy-makers had no first-hand experience of the places they were dealing with, and often worked by analogy with more familiar issues: thus the constant fear, for example, that South Africa would become 'another Ireland'. Such analogies could prove radically misleading. Domestic political issues also caused divisions between and among the parties: again, Irish affairs were significant, producing fractures among the British political elite that influenced the degree of support available in Cabinet and Parliament for various African policies. Ireland could thus set the range of policy options available in Africa. Above all, partly due to a lack of reliable information from overseas, and partly due to the interrelated nature of a whole range of geo-strategic considerations, the course of imperial affairs was always particularly unpredictable. The **official mind** might set out to secure a particular policy goal, only to find itself overwhelmed by unanticipated problems.[20]

Picking up and extending the arguments that they had first developed in 'The Imperialism of Free Trade', Robinson and Gallagher claimed in *Africa and the Victorians* that British territorial expansion had little to do with any specific interest, economic or otherwise, in Africa in and of itself. Rather, 'the decisive motive behind late-Victorian strategy in Africa was to protect the all-important stakes in India and the East'.[21] British policy-makers were determined to retain control of the sea-routes to the Far East, due to the broad economic and strategic importance of India to Britain. Two places in Africa were key: the Suez Canal to the north, and the Cape of Good Hope to the south. Traditionally, the Canal had been protected from Russian expansionism by the Ottoman

Empire (propped up by Britain for this purpose) and by a carefully brokered agreement between Britain and France to preserve Egypt's neutrality. The Cape had meanwhile been safeguarded by a strong British settler presence, capable of exerting economic and political predominance over the long-established and potentially rebellious Dutch settlers at the coast and in the two Boer republics in the interior, the Transvaal and the Orange Free State. However, during the 1880s two developing 'peripheral crises' destroyed both these mechanisms for protecting Britain's routes to the East.

The first peripheral crisis resulted from the continuing collapse of the Ottoman Empire, which left Egypt badly exposed to Russian expansion, and from growing European trade with and investment in Egypt, which precipitated the bankruptcy of the Egyptian state. Reluctantly, from 1880 onwards British policy-makers began to involve themselves more directly in Egyptian affairs, for fear that the French would otherwise intervene on their own. As the subsequent Egyptian national revolt degenerated into anti-European violence, W. E. Gladstone's Liberal government desperately sought to agree a coordinated course of action with the Ottomans and the French. When this proved unattainable, in the summer of 1882 the British government reluctantly authorized a unilateral military intervention, in the hope of quickly restoring stable government and then withdrawing. 'They had no long-term plan to occupy Egypt and saw no strategic need to do so. They had muddled and drifted with events. Each fateful step seemed to be dictated by circumstances rather than will.'[22] Subsequently, the breakdown of the old agreement with France to preserve the neutrality of Egypt, and the failure to find any Egyptian collaborators willing and able to restore the old order, left Britain mired in the position of a long-term occupying power. This was precisely the outcome that Gladstone's government had sought to avoid.

The defence of the Suez Canal now seemed to rest on continued British occupation of Egypt, making withdrawal impossible. Indeed, according to Robinson and Gallagher, Gladstone's Conservative successor Lord Salisbury feared that the French would try to drive Britain out of Egypt by gaining control of the headwaters of the Nile. If the French dammed the Nile then the Egyptian economy would collapse. Even if this was a remote possibility, Salisbury still felt obliged progressively to extend British authority up the Nile and into East Africa over the following decade-and-a-half. The French compensated by expanding aggressively in West Africa, and the Germans exploited the opportunity provided by the breach between the British and the French to extract colonial concessions of their own. Gladstone's occupation of Egypt thus unwittingly set in motion the wider partition of the continent.[23] Policy-makers only pondered later whether Britain might trade with or invest in the new African colonies, and perhaps thus secure recompense for the bother and expense of governing and defending them.

The second peripheral crisis identified by Robinson and Gallagher occurred in southern Africa, and was the consequence of the discovery of rich gold deposits in the Transvaal. This mineral strike made the Boer republic the economic powerhouse of the region. British policy-makers feared that, instead of the Cape-dominated, pro-British federation that they had long hoped would emerge in the region, the Transvaal would, due to its new economic influence, eventually turn all of southern Africa against the empire. The region would spin out of Britain's orbit, and possibly be drawn into that of a rival great power such as Germany. Initially, the British government saw Cecil Rhodes as the most effective available counterweight to the Boers. Rhodes promised to use his own great wealth, derived from diamond- and gold-mining interests, to bankroll British settler expansion into what became Rhodesia (later Zimbabwe and Zambia), thus hopefully returning economic leadership to the Cape. Rhodes's dreams came to nothing, however, and in 1895 a planned military coup and British revolt in the Transvaal misfired badly, destroying Rhodes's political career in the process. It was the British Colonial Secretary, Joseph Chamberlain, who now took charge. Seeking to ensure that a strong, British-dominated South Africa remained a bulwark of empire, Chamberlain pushed events to a crisis. Chamberlain hoped to break the Boers' power by forcing them to give British settlers in Johannesburg a share in government. Instead, the Boers opted for war. Chamberlain still hoped that the eventual British victory in the South African War of 1899–1902 would cement Britain's interests in the region. In the long term, as with British policy in Egypt, this proved a 'grand illusion'. South Africa would indeed slip from the empire's grasp, as Cape Dutch and Boers came together under the banner of a powerful, white-supremacist, and anti-British 'Afrikaner' nationalism.[24]

► Sub-imperialism and geopolitics

Robinson and Gallagher presented a remarkably subtle and persuasive account of the policy-making process, undermining earlier attempts to build simple, all-encompassing theories of imperialism. They showed that policy-making was seldom an entirely rational process, that decisions had often not originally been taken for the reasons later used to justify them, and that the outcomes of policy-making sometimes bore little relation to initial hopes or intentions.

Much of the debate generated by Robinson and Gallagher's writings focused on their arguments about the continuities in Victorian policy-making. A number of critics refuted their claim that mid-Victorian free-trader policy-makers could be described in any meaningful way as 'imperialists'. Others suggested that **informal empire** was a misnomer, that it implied Britain had more control over affairs in places like Latin America and China than the evidence actually suggested. Here, Robinson and Gallagher's sweeping and imprecise definition of what constituted 'imperialism' proved a significant analytical weakness.[25] In contrast, their broader account of policy-making and their concept of the **official mind** have fared much better.

Following Robinson and Gallagher's dazzling, mobile assault on earlier theories of imperialism, David Fieldhouse carried out a systematic mopping-up operation. Like Robinson and Gallagher, he argued that the quickening of the pace of territorial annexations after 1880 did not reflect any essential changes in the British economy or British policy, or indeed in wider European economies or policies. Marxist arguments about 'monopoly capitalism', derived from the German and to a lesser extent American cases, were hardly applicable to the economies of Britain or most of the other imperial powers, where industrial concentration remained relatively limited. Similarly, there was scant evidence for the existence of 'surplus capital' requiring safe havens in tropical colonies: there was little correlation between where different European countries invested overseas, and where they held and established colonies. Britain placed the bulk of its overseas investments outside its colonies (some imperial powers, such as Russia and the US, were significant recipients of British capital), and what it did invest in the empire went overwhelmingly to the old settler colonies and to India, not to the new tropical colonies which had supposedly been created as places to deposit surplus capital. Countries like France, Germany, and the US meanwhile invested miniscule amounts in their colonies, and imperial powers like Russia, Italy, Portugal, and Spain were actually net importers of capital. Neither could Fieldhouse find conclusive evidence to prove that, after 1880, European business interests had started to lobby for territorial expansion with increased intensity, or that European policy-makers had fallen victim to the machinations of any such group.[26]

Fieldhouse did acknowledge that European commercial involvement in Africa, Asia, and the Pacific had grown throughout the nineteenth century. However, before 1880 this did not encourage much in the way of formal imperial expansion, because non-European regimes seemed capable of delivering everything that European enterprise required. Forceful intervention in China, to establish the treaty port system, was exceptional, and even here European involvement did not lead to extensive territorial control. Rather, Fieldhouse argued, two things drove British territorial expansion before 1880. First, British governments annexed territory in areas where large-scale white settlement was taking place: Australia, New Zealand, and the Cape Colony in southern Africa. However, they subsequently granted those territories self-government (see Chapter 2), so long-term direct control could hardly have been of overwhelming importance to them. Second, in some places British military or civilian officers 'on the spot' were able to push colonial frontiers outwards in pursuit of local strategic ends. This **sub-imperialism** was often motivated by the desire to protect existing colonies from perceived external threats on their borders. India provided a prime example. During the nineteenth century, policy-makers in Calcutta were determined to see off any challenge to British 'paramountcy', partly in order to protect trade links, but mainly for military and strategic reasons. Policy-makers in London generally fell in with their wishes.

> By the mid-century Indian safety was thought to require British naval predominance throughout the Indian Ocean, and neutral buffer states or British possessions on all landward frontiers. By 1880 the Suez Canal had become another necessary safeguard for India, and in the next decade East Africa joined the list.[27]

As Robinson and Gallagher had suggested, empire spawned empire.

After 1880, Fieldhouse argued, economic factors played a significant but secondary role in British and European territorial expansionism. European commerce and finance in Africa, Asia, and the Pacific did not *directly* drive European policy-making towards annexation, but it did play an important part in progressively undermining local state structures. The cumulative effects of European enterprise were to bring about a whole series of peripheral crises in the two decades after 1880, leaving European governments to decide on how they should respond. Like Robinson and Gallagher, Fieldhouse argued that policy-makers were generally reluctant to resort to annexation. The British occupied Egypt, and the French Tunisia, only after local state structures had collapsed, and when other powers threatened to rush into the vacuum.[28] Similar local crises elsewhere, caused partly by the cumulative impact of European enterprise, and partly by the machinations of sub-imperialists 'on the spot', hastened the collapse of non-European state structures and endangered key European commercial and particularly strategic interests. European international rivalries then often led policy-makers to annex, fearing that other powers would do so if they did not.

Together, Robinson and Gallagher and Fieldhouse thus assigned economic forces a much less central role in explaining the 'why' and 'how' of British imperial expansion. British and European commerce and finance might have created peripheral crises, which in turn forced reluctant statesmen to annex territory as non-European polities collapsed. But British statesmen did not embark on imperial expansion in expectation of vast profits for the nation, or at the behest of manipulative groups of traders, investors, or financiers. Viewing the broad sweep of British imperial history, Ronald Hyam has argued that the flaw in 'all theories of economic determinism' is that 'they are not grounded in any real understanding of how governments think. Decisions are not taken by trends or abstract phenomena, but by individuals in very small inner groups.'[29] In Britain, the social elite from which these groups were drawn received little formal training before undertaking this role (the public schools and old universities offered at best a generalist's training), and often understood little about the workings of the economy. They tended to look down on those representatives of commercial interest groups who sought to influence their decisions, regarding them as their social inferiors. They were often able to ignore or override troublesome sub-imperialists on the frontier. Rather than pursuing well-thought-out, programmatic policy objectives, they found themselves reacting to immediate problems. They worked with a rough-and-ready set of calculations concerning the national interest, and considered imperial issues in the widest of frameworks. They thought primarily in terms of **geopolitics**, of global balances of strategic and military power. Economic considerations were not absent, but were generally subordinate. The inner elite also worried endlessly about the loss of 'prestige', the elusive stuff of diplomacy that could be built up through the decisive and successful use of power, but quickly eroded by the failure to act and the loss of initiative. Policy-makers sought to hold what they had, and reluctantly agreed to expand existing frontiers where this seemed necessary to ward off potential challengers. Salisbury complained of advisers who pressed him to 'annex the moon in order to prevent its being appropriated by the planet Mars'.[30]

▶ Decolonization

For Hyam, these insights can also help explain how and why Britain granted self-government to its former colonies during the twentieth century and thus wound up its formal empire. Hyam argues that the British policy-making elite viewed **decolonization** primarily through the lens of **geopolitics**. National economic interests did not play a decisive role in the decision to transfer power, because it seldom seemed necessary to retain direct political control in order to protect those interests, and because businessmen themselves 'exercised no influence on decolonization'.[31] This may be somewhat of an exaggeration: business interests did seek to present their case to policy-makers, who did make time to listen even if they did not necessarily do as they were asked. Nevertheless, it seems broadly true that such individual interests exerted little real influence over the course of **decolonization**. This was partly because **decolonization** did not necessarily seem to work against the best interests of British businesses in Africa and Asia. While colonial rule might have brought a stable and predictable political and economic climate, good for business, it also meant the imposition of numerous restrictions on the activities of British firms. Independent successor regimes might be less stable, but they were also far less managerial in their approach to the economy, and offered British businesses many financial incentives to invest as well as a more permissive regulatory regime in which to operate.[32]

Hyam argues that, in the wake of the First World War, the main goal for policy-makers was to protect the British empire from future foreign aggression by shoring up its military and strategic position. After the Second World War policy-making was similarly influenced by a concern to preserve British prestige. Contemporaries tried to calculate where Britain's interests would best be served by forcefully resisting those who sought its retreat, and where in contrast it would be better to withdraw sooner rather than later. Often, this came down to a calculation about whether it would be possible to hand power to a well-disposed, non-Communist successor regime that had a reasonable prospect of remaining in the saddle after the British withdrew. In Malaya, for example, it seemed necessary to suppress Communist insurgents by fighting an extended counter-insurgency campaign before handing power to a Malay-dominated successor state. Several other, more general geopolitical shifts also influenced decision-makers in this period. Once the transfer of power in India was complete, a multitude of old strategic interests suddenly disappeared. Just as the possession of India had made the projection of British power across a much wider territory seem necessary, so the loss of India made a much more general imperial withdrawal appear possible and even desirable. Similarly, the retreat of the French and Belgians from empire (and the seeming inevitability of an eventual Portuguese withdrawal) left the British reluctant to remain the sole colonial power at a time when 'imperialism' and 'colonialism' were becoming terms of abuse in Cold War politics and the new international forum of the United Nations. [33]

In contrast to Hyam, Ronald Robinson and Wm. Roger Louis suggested that British policy-makers took a more active role, retaining the diplomatic initiative to a considerable extent throughout the period of **decolonization**. Indeed, Robinson and Louis wrote of the 'imperialism of decolonization': they used this phrase as a means to highlight the aggressive imperial drives behind British policy in the decades after the Second World War, and to emphasize the continuities with earlier phases of British policy-making. Just as the concept of the 'imperialism of free trade' had been used to connote the long-term survival of trends and principles in policy-making throughout the nineteenth century, the 'imperialism of decolonization' suggested that those threads also connected the nineteenth and twentieth centuries.

For Robinson and Louis, the aim of British policy-makers after the Second World War was to convert **formal empire** into **informal empire**, and thus re-apply the age-old wisdom of the **official mind**. **Decolonization** was the means to achieve this: policy-makers granted Britain's Asian and African colonies self-government in the belief that this was the best means to secure British strategic and economic interests, as had been the case with the settler colonies in the nineteenth century. Policy-makers also hoped to perpetuate British imperial influence by drawing on American support, as part of the broader Cold War alliance. American resources would be used to supplement British power overseas and to continue the work of binding peripheral areas into the world economy. **Neocolonialism**, the imposition of continued imperial control under the guise of independence, was not just a figment of the imagination of colonial nationalists: it was more or less what British policy-makers were aiming at. For a time at least, British policy-makers thus retained the initiative, making new bargains with local collaborators, and deploying force where necessary to crush resistance. Ultimately however, as Robinson and Louis emphasized, there developed a substantial gap between British imperial aspirations and achievements. British influence was progressively undermined as the nation's economic and military resources dwindled, and as US power gradually seeped into the resulting vacuum. 'Under the shadow of cold war, a once British Empire modulated strategically into an Anglo-American field of influence, and thence into a predominantly American commitment.' In the final reckoning, the belief that imperial influence could be retained acted as a comforting delusion, smoothing the path to the dissolution of empire.[34]

If all these accounts have one obvious weakness, it is their tendency to exaggerate the importance of the **official mind** and the degree of control it exerted over the **decolonization** process. As Stephen Howe has argued, there is a strong case for widening the scope of the historiography of **decolonization** 'to include parties, pressure groups, business interests, and the currents of public opinion', as well as the influence of African and Asian nationalism.[35] **Decolonization** awaits the construction of convincing overarching concepts and theories to aid historical analysis. This is perhaps all to the good, as it has recently been revealed that a potentially significant body of archival evidence concerning British policy-making and the activities of colonial states 'on the spot' (particularly the use of coercive violence) may have been hidden from scrutiny. Material that has now been located relating to the British suppression of the Mau Mau movement in Kenya contains detailed evidence of the 'administration of torture and substantive allegations of abuse', as well as the use of forced labour.[36] At the time of writing, it is not clear how much of this material exists, or what exactly it contains. But future historians of British **decolonization** will have to grapple more closely with the role played by the violent suppression of African and Asian resistance at the end of empire.[37]

▶ Gentlemanly capitalism

The most significant recent attempt to present a single overarching theory of imperial expansion and contraction is contained in P. J. Cain and A. G. Hopkins' *British Imperialism*, published in two volumes in 1993 and subsequently republished in a single-volume second edition.[38] This ambitious work of synthesis, mainly focusing on the period between 1850 and 1950, attempts to reveal the deep-seated economic forces and relationships that shaped the British empire and Britain's engagement with the wider world. In particular, Cain and Hopkins seek to show how, under the international free trade order, market mechanisms operated to structure imperial connections between different sectors of the British economy and the colonies. They also present a general argument about the forces driving imperial expansion, about decision-making and where the power to shape policy was located.

To some extent, Cain and Hopkins seek to rehabilitate Hobson's arguments about the central importance of finance and financiers in British empire-building. They also echo John Bright's quip that the empire was 'a gigantic system of out-door relief for the aristocracy of Great Britain', and Schumpeter's claim that empire reflected the continued influence of pre-modern elements in European society. For Schumpeter, empire was the result not of the triumph of capitalism, but rather of its incomplete dominance and of the continuing influence of the aristocracy. Empire gave the aristocracy the chance to demonstrate their martial pre-eminence, and reinforced the socially conservative influence of nationalism and militarism.[39]

Cain and Hopkins have modified Schumpeter's argument somewhat, claiming that Britain's imperial expansion resulted from the blending of 'traditional' and 'modern' elements in British society. Agricultural, landowning elites enjoyed massive prestige and political power in Britain. During the eighteenth century they bolstered their own wealth and influence, and that of the British state, through overseas expansion. During the nineteenth century, as agricultural fortunes entered into a long-term decline, the landowning elite forged a new alliance with groups in the 'service sector' of the economy, in the worlds of commerce and especially finance. This resulted in the emergence of a new 'gentlemanly capitalist' elite, sharing traditional aristocratic cultural values and focused geographically in the South of England and particularly in the City of London. The City helped channel aristocratic fortunes into safe investments in the empire, which were then further protected by the British state through the establishment of **formal** and **informal empire**. These arguments echo Hobson's claim that privileged elites had used state power to protect their own interests.

For Cain and Hopkins, the state served the needs of the gentlemanly capitalist elite because those who ran the state were essentially a part of that elite.

Northern, industrial interests were meanwhile marginalized, able to secure little access to the world of policy-making. The result was the creation of a vast international sterling trading system, maintaining the wealth and power of financiers and aristocrats, and relying on British imperial muscle to reshape overseas economies as necessary to fit in with the system's requirements. Britain's free trade policies were maintained to benefit the world of finance, not manufacturing. Free trade was necessary if other countries were to export goods to Britain and earn sufficient sterling to service their debts. The British government intervened, diplomatically or militarily, wherever and whenever investments were threatened or defaults on debts seemed likely. Sound finances were the main aim of colonial governance, putting the requirements of British investors above those of colonial subjects.

Cain and Hopkins's theory marks a self-conscious turn away from the 'peripheral' theories associated with Robinson and Gallagher and Fieldhouse, and back towards a 'metropolitan' explanation for empire. Cain and Hopkins also reject the idea of an **official mind** seeking to protect national economic and strategic interests, and instead renew the claim that empire was driven by the economic requirements of particular interest groups in British society. In the case of the Scramble for Africa, for example, Cain and Hopkins deny that strategic considerations were uppermost in the minds of British policy-makers. They argue instead that the need to protect British investments and promote British financial interests lay behind decisions made in Egypt, South Africa, and across the rest of the continent.

However, other historians have registered numerous objections to Cain and Hopkins's theory. To many, it seems like a step backwards towards a universal, mono-causal, economically determinist theory of imperial expansion and contraction. Some have questioned Cain and Hopkins's model of British society, asking whether there really was a close and long-lasting alliance between aristocratic and financial interests, or whether the City was as monolithic, and as gentlemanly, as Cain and Hopkins believe. The concept of gentlemanly capitalism might also exaggerate just how marginalized manufacturing interests were in the world of policy-making.[40] Other historians have argued that the territories of the British empire were so diverse that any unified, overarching theory such as that offered by Cain and Hopkins can have only limited explanatory power. Rather than acting as the mere playground of a gentlemanly capitalist elite, the empire offered varied opportunities to different elements within a vast and disparate array of economic and other interests, each of which had their own particular imperial agendas and reasons for supporting imperial expansion or consolidation.[41] Here, it is worth noting that Cain and Hopkins' picture of the **periphery**, of the varying conditions and constellations of power and interest in the colonies, is much more sketchily rendered compared with their detailed study of conditions in Britain itself.

Finally, and perhaps most significantly for our purposes here, the empirical underpinnings of Cain and Hopkins's account of the political influence exerted by the gentlemanly capitalist elite seem weak. The concept of gentlemanly capitalism is prominently set out at the beginning of their study, but is not then interrogated rigorously in their subsequent analysis of the relationship between policy-making and the economics of empire. Cain and Hopkins tend to write about general impulses behind imperial policy, while offering only sparse evidence for direct City influence over the making of specific decisions. They tend to assume that a gentlemanly capitalist consensus made it unnecessary for the City to intervene in the policy-making process on a day-to-day or even occasional basis, that the logic of the economic requirements of gentlemanly capitalism naturally translated into policy. Yet other historians have doubted whether City financiers and policy-makers in London and the colonies marched together in lock-step. Ultimately, Cain and Hopkins offer not a proven account of the forces driving British imperial expansion and contraction, but a series of assertions as to how their theory of gentlemanly capitalism should work out in a number of different cases. They have left it to subsequent historians to prove or disprove these assertions through more extensive empirical research.[42]

▶ Pluralist explanations of empire

As John Gallagher argued,

> All theories to explain the growth of imperialism have been failures. Here and there on the mountain of truth lie the frozen bodies of theorists, some still clutching their ice-picks, others gripping their hammers and sickles. All perished; and most of them because they believed they could find some single cause or factor which could satisfactorily explain imperialism's efflorescence in the later nineteenth century. We may expect a similar fate for those who want a monocausal explanation of its fall. They may climb hopefully, but they will not arrive. The task when considering domestic constraints and international pressures is not to rank them, but to join them up, to identify ways in which one set of forces worked on the other in critical situations.[43]

Some of the more recent and most convincing large-scale historical studies of imperial expansion and contraction have followed this sage advice. They have offered pluralist, multi-causal explanations which seek to show the interaction of different historical actors, rather than to reduce imperial history to a mono-causal account of the past. While retaining Robinson and Gallagher's emphasis on the state, international rivalries, and geopolitical contests, these recent accounts have stressed that we need to see empire as the product of a complex interplay of multiple forces, interests, and agents, moving beyond the limits of the **official mind**.

Christopher Bayly has made this case forcefully when examining British expansion in the late eighteenth and early nineteenth centuries. As Bayly points out, alongside the Scramble for Africa this represented the other great period of British empire-building, and probably the more significant one in terms of the scope of population and resources involved. British expansion in this period was focused in South Asia.[44] Although this new empire was managed primarily by a commercial organization, the East India Company, Bayly argues that commercial interests were not in themselves what drove expansion. This seeming paradox reflected the fact that, because of its need to mobilize considerable military resources, the East India Company had come to operate more like a state than a commercial enterprise.

For Bayly, empire-building in this period was a product of intense and long-drawn-out rivalries between European states. These rivalries pushed up military expenditure at a time of falling revenues. Tapping overseas resources was a way for European states to balance the books.[45] By the late eighteenth century the East India Company no longer concerned itself primarily with trade, but had become a mechanism for squeezing enormous revenues from Indian peasants, to pay for the military force that simultaneously suppressed colonial unrest and allowed Britain to fight off rival Asian and European state- and empire-builders. Once entrenched territorially and militarily, and placed in a position where further conflict with surrounding Asian powers was inevitable, the British presence in India constituted a powerful agent of **sub-imperialism**, further stimulating processes of territorial expansion.[46]

Further supporting his argument that British expansion in India was not motivated directly by commercial considerations, Bayly points out that the overseas penetration of Britain's industrial economy came after eighteenth-century territorial expansion in India. Thus empire may have stimulated British industrialization, but cannot have been caused by it. Echoing Schumpeter, Bayly argues that British expansion was not driven by the industrial bourgeoisie searching for profit abroad, but by a conservative aristocracy seeking to reinforce its dominance at home. Like Robinson and Gallagher, Bayly also acknowledges the role of the irrational in policy-making: empire in India may have been pursued out a sense of broad national interest, but it was acquired 'in an atmosphere of panic and providential messianism', rather than as the result of cool and dispassionate analysis.[47]

In explaining subsequent British imperial expansion, Bayly devotes much attention to the nature of state structures. In the mid-eighteenth century, he argues, from a global perspective state structures were variegated and patchy in their influence. States tended to intervene in the workings of society and economy as little as possible. In some parts of the world, little in the way of effective state authority existed at all. However, during the French Revolutionary and Napoleonic Wars European state structures became much more powerful and interventionist, capable of mobilizing their subjects and their resources more comprehensively and turning them to more deadly military purposes. 'The slowly emerging patriotic and information-rich state ... was quite suddenly inflated to a massive degree. It grew gargantuan in its ideological ambitions, its global reach, and its demand for military and civilian labour.'[48] Larger and more effective European state structures provided not just the means but also the incentive for territorial expansion: by capturing the revenues of non-European subjects, European states could help fund their swollen military machines.[49]

Bayly also links nineteenth-century empire-building to the new currents of nationalism running through British and other European societies. In order to mobilize their subjects more effectively, and maintain domestic order, states sought to harness developing national identities. This 'official nationalism' in turn gave empire-building added impetus and strengthened international rivalries. Nationalist resistance in Egypt and the Transvaal meanwhile prompted an imperial backlash at the century's end.[50]

John Darwin has similarly emphasized the 'astonishing portfolio of motivations and capacities' that drove British overseas expansion in the nineteenth century: ideologies of free trade, utilitarianism, evangelical Christianity, and anti-slavery; an economy in which both production and consumption were burgeoning and a powerful finance sector was developing; population growth and emigration; the creation of a formidable navy; and an army strengthened by the possession of Indian military resources.[51] These varied influences worked their way out in different places in diverse ways. As a result, theories which seek to provide one central explanation for British imperial expansion 'do insufficient justice to the contingency of Victorian empire-making'.[52]

For Darwin, contingency also helps us understand the limits of British power and the metropolitan state's inability to impose its will across the globe. Darwin suggests that **informal empire** might have reflected a reluctant acknowledgement that the British presence could go no further, rather than a conscious avoidance of formal rule. Britain relied on **informal empire** not out of choice, but because it was not strong enough to impose formal control everywhere that it might serve British interests to do so.

Darwin also stresses that **informal empire** was a capacious category encompassing a very wide range of different types of unequal relationship. In some cases private interests were able to impose British requirements by themselves. In other instances greater state intervention was required to set a clear framework for British dominance. Often, policy-makers simply muddled through, improvising on the hoof in response to unpredictable and unstable local circumstances. Policy-makers might nurture a sense of broad national interests, but 'the circumstances and pressures which buffeted decision-makers made it very difficult to translate these broad desiderata into any consistent set of diplomatic or imperial principles, let alone practice'.[53] A whole panoply of different types of **informal empire** might be established or imposed in sequence, without the application of any set of clear overarching principles, and with widely varying success rates in terms of protecting British interests.

All this gave sub-imperialists 'on the spot' considerably more power than policy-makers in London to shape the pace and scope of territorial expansion. Darwin emphasizes 'the incoherence of colonial expansion and the inability of the metropole to exert consistent influence except where the bridgeheads of occupation were weak or dependent upon its financial or military aid'.[54] As traders, officials, settlers, and missionaries built up resources on the ground in the colonies and supporters at home in Britain, some 'bridgeheads' became more able than others to impose their will on London. For Darwin, the Scramble for Africa was not driven by any British strategic master-plan aimed at protecting Egypt: rather, 'local factors and sub-imperialist forces made the running: not the official mind'.[55] He concludes that

> late Victorian governments did not annex so widely in tropical Africa because this was the only way of maintaining their mid-Victorian interests. Nor did they espouse pessimistic new doctrines of relative decline. They annexed for the same reasons as mid-Victorians governments: because local British interests pressed them to do so and, in the absence of powerful diplomatic, financial or military objections, the will to refuse was lacking.[56]

► Conclusions

From a world-historical perspective, empires may be a simple consequence of 'the political logic of enrichment by expansion'.[57] Yet once we move from this abstract approach to a more specific type of historical analysis, it quickly becomes clear that such a statement raises more questions than it answers. Theories about the expansion and contraction of the British empire have competed to explain who was enriched by empire-building, and how those who benefited from empire might have influenced the policy-making process. Yet it is not a simple case of following the money. Early Radical Liberal and Marxist accounts of imperialism argued that empire had enriched capitalists and financiers, and that those interest groups must therefore have been the ones driving governments into overseas expansion. However, when historians began to comb their way through the archives, they found little evidence to suggest that commercial interest groups had captured policy-makers and forced them to annex territory overseas. Politicians and civil servants had worked according to much broader definitions of British overseas interests, and had sought to secure what they saw as national economic and geopolitical goals. Although Cain and Hopkins have identified the City of London, and a broader group of gentlemanly capitalists, as the prime movers behind British imperialism, again the archives seem to offer little support to such an overarching, economic-determinist account. A whole range of different groups sought to advance and defend imperial agendas, sometimes with the backing of the British government, and sometimes at odds with it. Concepts such as the **official mind** and **informal empire** are helpful in explaining how this process of political contest and negotiation shaped the building, maintenance, and disintegration of the British empire. But no mono-causal theory can offer a persuasive account of the motivations behind British imperial advance and retreat.

Much of the debate generated by the concepts and theories examined in this chapter ultimately revolves around the relationship between the state and imperial expansion. Historians have disagreed about who controlled the British state, how impartial it was in mediating between different interest groups, and whose needs it really served. More broadly, some have argued that empire was essentially a product of the development of 'modern' state structures and their patchy growth across the globe, and was a means for those state structures to strengthen and replicate themselves. One of the significant implications of the work of Robinson and Gallagher, and of Fieldhouse, was that formal imperial rule was essentially a means of creating states in areas where they were weak or absent. As Darwin has put it more recently, 'Empires arose from the maldistribution of state-building resources'.[58] Formal colonial rule was only undertaken where the state structures necessary for European enterprise had become fatally undermined, or were lacking altogether, generating peripheral crises that eventually led to annexation. Subsequently, one of the key consequences and legacies of both informal influence and formal rule was the creation of new state structures. As Robinson and Gallagher argued,

> Once entry had been forced into Latin America, China and the Balkans, the task was to encourage stable governments as good investment risks, just as in weaker or unsatisfactory states it was considered necessary to coerce them into more co-operative attitudes.[59]

The implication of these arguments is that European overseas expansion was not really about anything as superficial as the economic interests of particular groups or the racial prejudices of Europeans. Rather, it might be better understood as a mere epiphenomenon, generated by the more profound global transformations (prevalent in Europe and throughout the world, not just in colonized areas) that encouraged the development of the modern state.[60] Fieldhouse even suggested that the formal European empires should be regarded as a 'temporary expedient'. They lasted only as long as was necessary to create modern state structures, and then dissolved themselves: 'empire eventually provided its own solvent'.[61]

Such arguments bring with them implications that some historians have found deeply unappealing. These arguments might lead us to conclude that, although European commercial enterprise catalysed the disintegration of non-European state structures, it was really the inherent weakness of those structures that forced European powers reluctantly to build formal empires. Similarly, we might reason that it was the success of those empires in building strong new colonial state structures that ultimately made **decolonization** possible. For some scholars, these sorts of claims carry with them the unpalatable suggestion that non-Europeans were responsible for the fact that European powers had to establish empires, and that the European empires were ultimately successful in their aims and willingly and virtuously abolished themselves when those aims had been realized. It is worth bearing these ideas, and the objections to them, in mind as we turn in the next chapter to examining theories and concepts that seek to explain the nature and consequences of colonial rule.

2 Control

▶ Who ran the British empire?

Why would we need a theory to understand how the British empire was controlled? Empires, we might imagine, are a peculiarly centralizing, intrusive form of government. The imperial **core** power seeks to direct the affairs of the **periphery** from the centre: an empire is thus often assumed to be 'an administrative monolith, a leviathan that was capable of repressing all opposition'.[1] Yet, at least as far as the British empire was concerned, the reality was generally very different. The imperial state in London could certainly intervene in the affairs of the colonies when it seemed necessary to do so. Instructions and officials could be despatched to the colonies, new legislation passed, overarching economic policies imposed, and gunboats, troops, and (later) aircraft sent to perpetrate acts of exemplary violence against those who would resist. Nevertheless, the ability and willingness of the imperial state to control the affairs of the colonies in detail, or on a day-to-day basis, were strictly limited. Too much central intervention, funded by British taxpayers, threatened to consume any economic benefit that might be had from empire. British policy-makers thus insisted that, as far as possible, the colonies should pay for their own governance. To facilitate this, power was devolved to agents of empire working 'on the spot' in each colony: officials, soldiers and sailors, missionaries, white settlers, and indigenous collaborators.

There is thus no simple answer to the question 'who ran the British empire?' Power was diffuse, distributed in a seemingly haphazard but often (from a British perspective) highly effective and economical fashion. Key decisions were not necessarily made in London, or indeed even in the various colonial capitals. Those operating at the frontier could play a crucial role in improvising and implementing policy. This is why we need theories to help us understand how the British empire was controlled, and identify and comprehend overall patterns.

Thinking about how the British empire was governed means thinking about the state or, more accurately, about dispersed, diverse, and decentralized state structures. As Ronald Robinson noted, in the British empire 'there was no unified imperial state, but as many different kinds of empire with as many different connections with Britain as there were countries under her sway'.[2] Powers of government in the British empire were devolved and multiple, not centralized and monolithic. By 1914, with a population roughly the size of Greater London, Canada sustained ten of its own parliamentary systems (nine in the provinces, plus a federal government in Ottawa) to preside over internal affairs, while its external affairs – trade, defence, and diplomacy – remained subject to the oversight of the British parliament at Westminster.[3] In India, it sometimes seemed to be the conscious aim of British policy-makers to spread power out across a wide range of local, provincial, and all-India institutions. This in turn made it possible to admit Indians into some sort of role in government, without challenging British control over key strategic areas of the state or encouraging Indians to unite in nationalist political mobilization. Across the British empire, who controlled what was never a simple matter and often a subject for debate.

In this context, it is again useful to think about definitions. In writing about state power, some (but not all) historians draw a conscious and careful distinction between the meanings of the words 'imperial' and 'colonial'. 'Imperial' refers to the authority emanating from the London-based state apparatus in Whitehall and Westminster, and the coercive forces it was able to direct: the British Monarchy, Parliament and Cabinet; the Colonial Office, India Office, Foreign Office, and Treasury; the British Army, the Royal Navy, and so forth. 'Colonial' authority, on the other hand, refers to those elements of government and coercion that were based in the colonies themselves: governors and viceroys; colonial councils and assemblies; colonial civil servants; colonial army units, paramilitary police forces, and settler militias. Some of these colonial elements might have been despatched from London, and remained under London's notional control. However, in reality they often proved difficult to manage from either Westminster or Whitehall.

In an age when the rapid or regular movement of people and information was impossible, it could hardly have been otherwise. In the early nineteenth century, few policy-makers in London had any experience of the world beyond Europe. Later, railways and steamships made it easier for some to visit the colonies, and on their return to present themselves as experts with practical experience. However, their understanding of empire was often based on superficial impressions gathered during short stays overseas, and quickly became outdated. It was also difficult to generalize about the empire from experiences gathered in only one or two parts of it. Meanwhile, information and instructions travelled with frustrating slowness within the empire's boundaries. The net result was that policy-makers in London were reluctant to intervene actively in colonial affairs: 'the still waters of colonial administration, no matter what pestilence they might be breeding for the future, were better left absolutely undisturbed'.[4] The British Parliament at Westminster, and the Colonial Office and India Office in Whitehall, might have possessed legal authority over the colonies, and exploited various unofficial channels and contacts in order to increase their influence.[5] Yet they seldom sought to manage the detailed administration of the colonies, or succeeded in doing so.

Colonial governors, the men 'on the spot' sent out by the government from London to head the administration of day-to-day affairs in each colony, did play a more active role in the running of the colonies. But London could hardly keep its deputies on a short leash: again, slow and unreliable communications links made this impossible. Moreover, governors often had to accommodate the ideas and plans of colonial officials and judges who had been appointed by previous administrations, and of white planters and settlers who demanded and often succeeded in winning a role for themselves in the making of local policy. Later, new communications technologies including steamships, railways, and telegraphs made it possible, in theory, for London to exercise greater control over its agents in the colonies. However, across Asia and especially in Africa, new technologies were slow to penetrate beyond coastal regions into the interior. As Prime Minister Lord Salisbury lamented when considering the frontiers of British involvement in Egypt, in the 1890s it remained 'as difficult to judge what is going on in the Upper Nile Valley as to judge what is going on on the other side of the moon'.[6] Even as late as the 1940s, few colonial officials in Africa possessed typewriters, and many remained reluctant to incur the considerable expense of using the telegraph. Isolated districts could be many weeks' travel from the nearest telegraph or railway station.

When London sent men (and they were all men) to help administer such remote outposts of empire, it acknowledged that its civil servants and military commanders would effectively be operating on their own for much of the time. The colonial civil services thus recruited men they deemed 'cool under pressure and who possessed sufficient independence of mind to deal with crises'. However, this was also exactly the sort of person who, in acting on their own initiative, would likely be prone to overstep the bounds of their authority. London had to accept the unpredictable consequences of giving such people power.[7] David Fieldhouse's theory of **sub-imperialism**, encountered in Chapter 1, is thus relevant here if we wish to understand how the British empire was controlled. Colonial governors ('imperial pro-consuls' as they were sometimes called) could play a significant role in accelerating or retarding the pace at which colonial boundaries were pushed outwards, in determining the geographic thrust of expansion, and in shaping how policies were applied on the ground in specific circumstances.[8]

Yet few historians would see white colonial governors or civil servants as the sole motor driving colonial government. As Ronald Robinson argued, the real challenge for imperial historians lies in explaining 'how a handful of European pro-consuls managed to manipulate the polymorphic societies of Africa and Asia, and how, eventually, comparatively small, nationalist elites persuaded them to leave'.[9] Much depended on the willingness of non-European elites to work for and with their would-be imperial overlords.

This chapter first offers a critical analysis of the concept of the colonial state. It discusses various theories of colonial governance, and looks at some of the objections to those theories that have developed out of empirical research. After considering the argument that colonial governments were subservient to the interests of British business, the chapter goes on to discuss the concept of **collaboration**. Then, taking a cultural turn, it looks at theories of 'colonial knowledge', and at some of the work that has emerged to question those theories.

▶ The colonial state

As discussed in Chapter 1, some historians have suggested an intimate connection between the British empire (and other modern empires) and state building. According to this theory, the British established imperial territorial control in places where existing state structures were weak or collapsing and seemed incapable of fulfilling British economic and strategic requirements. Once a place had become a colony, British officials worked to build new and stronger state structures which would provide the stable and predictable tools of governance that British policy-makers and entrepreneurs required. The British then retreated from empire, more or less willingly, once sufficiently robust state structures had been created, and local collaborators found who would run those state structures in such a way as to safeguard British interests in the future. There are some significant problems with these arguments, as will be discussed below. However, usefully, they encourage us to think about what state structures were created in the British empire and how they operated.

In considering colonial governance, historians have often written about the 'colonial state'. This term is sometimes used in a reasonably straightforward fashion, simply to mean the various apparatus by which affairs were governed 'on the ground' in each colony. However, the term has also been used in a more particular way, to draw out a contrast with the concept of the modern European nation-state. Some historians believe that colonial states in Africa and Asia governed their subjects in a different way than European nation-states did. They argue that the colonial state was a specific type of state, which needs to be understood in a particular way.

During the nineteenth and twentieth centuries, British administrators often presented the colonial state as the unselfish, high-minded protector of its subjects. The British, it was claimed, were holding power as trustees until future generations were deemed capable of governing themselves. The British guarded their charges against tyrannical traditional rulers, slavers, and rapacious European business interests. Niall Ferguson has argued that there was a great deal of truth in this ideal of trusteeship. The British spread good governance, progressive modern institutions, even liberty, throughout their colonies. Empire was about exporting British-style state structures, and departing when that task had been achieved.[10]

However, other historians argue that colonial states were designed specifically to extract resources from the colonies for the benefit of the British **metropole**. This was their *raison d'etre*, and they were structured so as to make this work easier. As Eric Stokes put it, 'British power in India came to be regarded after 1800 as no more than an accessory, an instrument for ensuring the necessary conditions of law and order by which the potentially vast Indian market could be conquered for British industry.'[11]

According to this argument, colonial states actively re-shaped society and its associated legal, administrative, and information systems, so as to achieve the most effective forms of economic exploitation. Colonial states prioritized the interests of British enterprises or of the British economy more generally. They taxed subjects, built infrastructure (roads, bridges, railways, telegraphs, harbours, irrigation schemes, etc.), developed larger and more intrusive bureaucracies, surveyed and registered land, regulated and influenced the supply of labour and raw materials, and set up new and consistent legislative and judicial frameworks. The overall aim was to facilitate the creation of an outward-facing economy that maximized the exportation of food and raw materials to the imperial centre and the importation of the products of British industry. Moreover, colonial states were better able and more willing to deploy coercive force to achieve their ends than were nation-states in Europe. Joanna Lewis argues that in Kenya, for example, the colonial state was apt to use force in pursuit of economic and social change, and that the extreme violence meted out against Mau Mau insurgents in the 1950s was in line with this trend, not some sort of aberration.[12] Jürgen Osterhammel offers a pithy summary: 'The colonial state had two main functions: to secure control over the subjugated peoples and to create a framework for the economic utilization of the colony.'[13]

The violent, coercive, and authoritarian approach of colonial states would not have been acceptable had it been deployed to govern Britain itself. However, it has been argued that colonial states pioneered oppressive practices that were later brought back 'home' to sharpen the claws of the British state. Rather than make the colonial state more like the nation-state, empire thus made the British state more like a colonial state, importing economic managerialism and political tyranny and eroding domestic liberties.

Much thinking about the nature of the colonial state and the impact of empire on British ideas about governance derives from work on British rule in India. Adopting insights from the discipline of anthropology, Bernard Cohn argued that the British replaced an earlier Indian 'theatre of power' (involving spectacle and ritual, the personal charisma of the ruler, and various established forms of 'traditional' knowledge) with a new 'officializing' mode of colonial governance. British civil servants worked to measure, classify, categorize, institutionalize, and thereby control space, individuals, and groups in India. Cohn also argued that this process eventually influenced the nature of governance in Britain itself. State-building in Britain and India became intimately connected:

> the projects of state building in both countries – documentation, legitimation, classification, and bounding, and the institutions therewith – often reflected theories, experiences, and practices worked out originally in India and then applied in Great Britain, as well as vice versa.

Ideas about organizing the civil service, structuring public education, and placing the monarchy at the centre of public life flowed back and forth between India and Britain.[14] Jon Wilson has similarly shown how, in late eighteenth- and early nineteenth-century India, British administrators hastily improvised new, impersonal tools of governance which had not previously been deployed in Britain. Only later would Britons at home be governed in the same remote, rule-bound, and bureaucratic 'modern' fashion.[15]

The prospect that authoritarian practices pioneered in the colonies might be brought back home to Britain troubled Whigs and Liberals from the earliest days of British empire-building: perhaps the vast Indian army would even one day be shipped from Asia to impose tyranny on Britain itself.[16] As we have already seen in Chapter 1, one of J. A. Hobson's main objections to 'imperialism' was its anti-liberal domestic consequences. Hobson was also a keen critic of the exploitative nature of the colonial state, arguing that it had been developed as a tool of governance so as to serve European commercial interests. In order to access the commodities that they required from the tropics, European businesses had used the colonial state to extract forced labour from local populations, or to facilitate the importation of indentured labour from elsewhere.[17]

The idea that the colonial state was the tool of British commercial interests has clear affinities with the Radical Liberal and Marxist theories of imperialism discussed in Chapter 1. Yet, logically, we do not have to buy whole-heartedly into those theories to accept the claim that the colonial state served British commercial interests. Even if we bow to the accumulated wisdom of scholarship, and agree that the British empire did not expand at the behest of British business, this does not mean that commercial interests did not seek to benefit from empire once territorial expansion had taken place. Even if British rule was established for non-economic reasons, it is possible that European business interests were subsequently able to seize new opportunities and turn the new colonial state structures to their own ends. Nevertheless, many historians still question whether we can view colonial states as the straightforward tool of British capitalists, or even of British economic interests more generally.

▶ The varieties and limits of the colonial state

Any simplistic model that posited a universal form of colonial state would be fatally flawed, for it would of necessity ignore the wide variety of modes of governance that were established in different parts of the British empire. The central elements of colonial governance varied considerably from place to place, and changed significantly over time: 'to speak of the [Indian] Raj, at the height of its elaboration, in the same breath as the administrations of, say, Lesotho or Zanzibar is not unlike treating an elephant, an emu, and an egret as the same kind of creature because they are all animals'.[18] Colonial states governed in different ways, served a range of different interests, and, crucially, varied significantly in terms of their ability to reach down into and influence colonial economies, societies, and cultures. Different groups of colonial subjects were governed in different ways: to some extent this reflected and was legitimated in terms of perceived racial differences. But race was never the whole story when it came to colonial governance, as will be discussed in Chapter 3.

Britain's settler colonies are often left out of consideration entirely when historians discuss the nature of the colonial state. Yet this omission distorts our overall understanding of colonial rule. Settler colonies were particularly difficult to control from London, but generated especially effective forms of colonial governance. After early phases of more-or-less authoritarian rule by the representatives of Westminster and Whitehall (particularly pronounced in the Australian convict settlements), white settlers increasingly demanded and won the ability to govern themselves. Settler claims to a role in the making of policy were hard to resist. Settlers argued that they were Britons, and had carried with them overseas the rights of Britons to govern themselves. They had also brought to the colonies the methods of political lobbying and campaigning that were so familiar to policy-makers back in Britain. As a result of their effective agitation, settlers were increasingly brought into colonial advisory councils, ostensibly to assist the London-appointed governor, but increasingly controlling budgets and seeking to direct policy. Policy-makers in London found it difficult, and ultimately counter-productive, to resist the current of change. During the second half of the nineteenth century Britain extended 'responsible self-government' across its settler empire. The settler colonies thus came to operate a system analogous to Westminster-style parliamentary government. Settlers built and controlled their own states, with London reserving overarching control only of their external affairs.[19]

For indigenous peoples, this generally meant the advent of a colonial state that turned a blind eye to (or actively participated in) settler violence perpetrated against them, and that fully supported policies of appropriation of land by settlers. If London had once offered indigenous peoples some protection from settlers, self-government henceforth made this constitutionally difficult or even impossible.

For settlers, meanwhile, self-government meant the creation of a state that was much more likely to intervene in direct and powerful ways in colonial economies, paying only lip service to the Victorian faith in laissez-faire. The state and the private sector worked together to drive a self-perpetuating process of rapid economic development, building new infrastructure and opening up land to white settlement. James Belich has labelled this potent combination the 'progress industry'.[20] The state intervened in the interests both of settlers and of investors back in Britain. Certainly, the colonial state had to protect British investment in order to ensure continued supplies of migrants and money. But even if this was 'dependent development', predicated on the requirements of the **metropole**, it seemed to work to the benefit of settlers too, providing the best means available to ensure rapid and sustained economic growth and high standards of living.[21]

Self-government meant that the settler colonies were held to Britain not by the supremacy of Westminster and Whitehall but by bonds of sentiment and of economic and military self-interest. For the British taxpayer, self-government had the added advantage of shifting the bill for colonial garrisons and government onto settler shoulders, even if Britain continued to provide the colonies with a large subsidy in the form of free naval defence. Robinson and Gallagher thus presented settler self-government as an effective variant of **informal empire**, requiring very little direct British intervention or expenditure, but safeguarding all of Britain's key requirements.[22]

Outside the settler colonies, the colonial state took a range of very different forms. No colony in Asia or tropical Africa, during the nineteenth century at least, was granted responsible self-government. The Westminster system of parliamentary government was deemed 'not for export' beyond the settler colonies. This way of thinking did not begin to change until the first half of the twentieth century in the case of India, and until after the Second World War insofar as the rest of the tropical empire was concerned.[23] Instead, British officials were sent out to staff the upper echelons of colonial civil services. In

India, local peasant revenues also supported a vast garrison state, composed of a substantial body of British (and Irish) officers and men, as well as Indian **sepoys**. The maintenance of the Indian army, which was placed at Britain's disposal for the defence of imperial interests elsewhere, was arguably the raison d'être of the *raj*. However, elsewhere in Asia, and across Africa, the size and military muscle of the colonial state was far less impressive.

Although white 'Europeans' (mainly British and Irish men) dominated the senior ranks of colonial civil services, Asians and Africans were not entirely excluded from participation in their own governance. In India, there were only around a thousand British civil servants. They relied on the presence of a huge army of Indian administrators, book-keepers, tax-collectors, and policemen, and on the state apparatus of the notionally autonomous (but ultimately subordinate) Indian princely states. By the early twentieth century, in response to pressure from increasingly organized, western-educated local elites, Indians were also being granted significant power in local government and provincial councils.

In other parts of Asia, and notably in Africa, the British meanwhile tried to lock indigenous participation in government into a decentralized, non-political system that became known as **indirect rule**. 'Traditional' leaders were appointed as the agents of colonial governance, collecting taxes and enforcing laws and received a boost to their own authority in the process. Little attempt was made to develop parliamentary-style assemblies in these places.[24]

This style of colonial governance was made possible by the fact that, in parts of Asia and across tropical Africa, the structures of the colonial state remained relatively weak, making few demands on most colonial subjects, and requiring only passive acquiescence rather than active support. There was little enthusiasm among British administrators in Whitehall or 'on the spot' in the colonies for creating forms of government that intervened more actively to promote British business or encourage economic and social development in general. The role of the state was conceived as being to superintend very gradual processes of change, to discharge a largely negative conception of trusteeship that involved protecting established economic, social, and cultural structures from disruption, rather than accelerating progress towards self-government or economic change. Thus, rather than actively promoting either the creation of a modern, British-style state, or ultra-exploitative forms of governance, in many places colonial rule may have encouraged stasis.

Only at a very late stage in the history of colonial governance did administrators seek to develop state structures in tropical Africa with the ability to transform local economies and societies. When they finally did so, they probably attempted to make the African colonial state look more like the British nation-state. As Joanna Lewis argues, in colonies such as Kenya British officials consciously sought during and after the Second World War to import British approaches to governance. Wartime and post-war British ideas about the welfare state were taken directly to the colonies, as officials 'applied more thoroughly to Africa what they knew about the working class in Britain and the experience of social engineering at home'.[25] Even then, however, their achievements generally fell far short of their ambitions for the transformative impact of the colonial state in what was to be its final incarnation.

Other historians have argued that the colonial state operated in a less cynical, and more chaotic, fashion than simple theories about its exploitative nature would have us believe. Civil servants were locked in 'bitter conflict' over policies and their intended outcomes: no clear thrust of policy could emerge as a result of this in-fighting.[26] Moreover, the public image of the incorruptible British colonial civil servant running an impartial and efficient state did not always match up to reality: Jonathan Saha has argued that the colonial state could sometimes even rely on corruption to function. Unofficial ways of doing things could be as important as formalities. White administrators could turn a blind eye to the misdeeds of subordinate non-white officials, a hidden instalment of the price paid for **collaboration**. For some colonial subjects, at least, 'everyday misrule was their lived experience of the state'. [27]

▶ **Capitalism and the colonial state**

Historians have also challenged the idea that the colonial state was simply the tool of British business interests, facilitating economic exploitation by private enterprise.

Southern Africa has been used as a key example by those who see the colonial state as the direct tool of capitalist interests. During the 1970s and 1980s, Marxist historians tended to argue that the South African state (following the creation of the Union of South Africa in 1910, which brought together the diverse British colonies and former Boer republics in the region) was subservient to the diamond and gold mining industry. According to this interpretation, the state transformed and impoverished the economic opportunities available to Africans, providing a framework of legislation that forced them into low-paid work in the mines. Although not as comprehensively disadvantaged, white labour was also shaped to the requirements of mining capital, in ways more direct and alienating than was the case in the other settler colonies or in Britain. Shula Marks and Stanley Trapido argued that this was in part the consequence of the South African War of 1899–1902, which they claim was fought to '[hasten] the development of a capitalist state, which would be more fully capable of fulfilling the demands of the mining industry'.[28] This state was able to intervene in the lives of its subjects in a much more direct and effective fashion, allowing it to reshape South African society. Its authority was strengthened by a powerful ideology of racial segregation. The process of creating this state was managed under the auspices of Sir Alfred (later Lord) Milner, the London-appointed British High Commissioner for Southern Africa (1897–1905). However, Marks and Trapido argued that Milner was really only a servant of the big mining companies. The colonial state in South Africa was thus subordinated to serving the interests of the mining industry, creating a modern bureaucracy, police force, judiciary, and education system, and favourable commercial and labour policy frameworks in order to increase the industry's profits.

However, other historians have questioned this reading of the South African War and of 'Milnerism'. They present the conflict not as the consequence of the machinations of the mining industry, but rather as the outcome of the aggressive, 'constructive imperialist' ideology of Milner himself and of key London-based policy-makers, most notably the British Colonial Secretary Joseph Chamberlain.[29] According to this view, the colonial state was far from the pliant tool of mining capitalism.

More broadly, in relation to other parts of the empire, historians have argued that Marxist accounts exaggerate the extent to which the colonial state could ride rough-shod over non-European interests. Colonial states were generally too weak to adopt a regime of all-out exploitation and thus risk destroying any legitimacy or consent they commanded in the eyes of their subjects.[30] As Ann Laura Stoler and Frederick Cooper have argued, the colonial state is better seen as a site contested by a whole range of economic and other interests, each seeking to win support for their own particular agenda. If we wish to understand how the colonial state functioned, we need to focus on the 'conflicting visions and practices of settlers, corporate leaders, and colonial officials, and on the struggles within plantations, mines, and factories in which economic and cultural power was deployed and deflected'.[31] There were similarities as well as differences between colonial states and European nation-states, in terms of how they dealt with the various economic disputes that they were supposed to referee. In colonial contexts, officials had to work with and through 'traditional' authorities, and could not afford to allow European capitalist interests to undermine those valuable collaborators. Sometimes political stability seemed more important than commercial profitability. Indeed, looking in detail at the activities of one British trading company in West Africa, David Fieldhouse has concluded that colonial officials often viewed British businesses with disdain. In some ways, British companies were the colonial state's rivals in a competition for local authority, not its allies. Colonial officials distrusted the motives of British businesses, saw them as potentially exploitative, and often preferred to mobilize African economic resources through state control rather than private enterprise. Colonial officials also often regarded British businessmen as their social inferiors, and did not necessarily mix with them in white expatriate society.[32]

As we have already seen, some historians have argued that colonial rule tended to encourage political stasis, rather than the emergence of either a British-style or an ultra-bureaucratic 'modern' state. This argument can be applied to economic interests, as well as to issues of governance. Thus, in the case of India, David Washbrook has argued that the colonial state was not in fact committed to serving British business interests: indeed, its policies 'can sometimes appear optimally designed to suppress economic activity whether undertaken by Indians or the great majority of Britons'.[33] Rather than opening up opportunities for business, the aim of policy-makers was to maximize the revenue extracted from Indian peasants. This income was not invested in infrastructure in order to stimulate economic expansion, as state revenues were in the settler colonies. There was no Indian 'progress industry'. Rather, peasant revenues were used to pay for the colonial state's enormous military machine, which consumed between 40 and 50 per cent of the government's income.[34] India was seen not as a land of business opportunities, but rather as a source of military power that could be used to open up and protect economic and strategic interests in other parts of the world.

The argument that the colonial state was an effective tool of capitalist interests may thus exaggerate its ability to exert a transformative influence over Asian and African societies and economies. As Douglas M. Peers argues, in the case of India, 'the end result of colonial rule was often the ossification and retardation of social and political institutions and the frustration of indigenous development'.[35] The Indian *raj* was hardly an agent of 'modernization'. In its desire to maximize revenues, it encouraged the 'sedentarization' and 'peasantization' of Indian society, obliging the population to remain on the land as taxable producers of agricultural goods. [36] Again, the contrast with the highly mobile and entrepreneurial societies created in the settler colonies is instructive.

In conclusion, these examples suggest that we need to avoid 'reifying' the colonial state: it should not be portrayed as a perfectly rational, pro-capitalist, all-intrusive leviathan. The reality was often different, particularly in Africa, where as we have seen the reach of the colonial state down into the vitals of society was relatively restricted. **Indirect rule** may have been a reflection not just of the 'traditionalizing' thrust of the colonial state, but also of the very limited capacities of the colonial state to transform or even much influence the societies it claimed to govern.

> Throughout the nineteenth century, the colonizing powers had cognizance of only a tiny proportion of judicial decisions in [colonial] societies, and had

much less of a grip on their revenues than they liked to believe. Their head counting and ethnographic surveys often had little practical impact, being less a guide to government than a hobby of scholar-administrators. Whole areas of the European colonial world, albeit divided by international treaties and maps into neat provinces, remained in the grip of greedy European financial interests, popular revolt, resistance to central authority, and the power of local chieftains until the very beginnings of decolonization itself in the 1940s ... The myths of today's historians about the power of the state often do no more than echo the aspirations of nineteenth-century rulers.[37]

In settler colonies where a great deal of British human and financial capital was invested, and in the tightly focused commercial enclaves in Asia where British trade was concentrated, the colonial state could prove formidable. Elsewhere, its ambitions and achievements were often much more modest than some theories of colonial governance would have us believe.

▶ Collaboration

Indeed, some historians have argued that the key characteristic of the colonial state was ultimately its reliance upon **collaboration** with non-European peoples. As we have seen, white colonial officials generally formed but a thin skin over broad and deep layers of Asian and African administrative muscle. White officials were too few in number to have discharged all of the functions required of even the most non-interventionist colonial state. Many of the activities of the state were in fact delegated to African and Asian low-level bureaucrats and 'traditional' leaders. The word 'collaborator' has negative connotations, particular through its associations in European politics during and after the Second World War. Nevertheless, most imperial historians have not used the word to denote a group of traitorous villains locked in conflict with heroic colonial nationalists. Rather, the concept of collaboration has been put to the less glamorous task of explaining how colonial rule functioned on an everyday level.

The concept of **collaboration** was developed during the late 1960s and early 1970s by the so-called 'Cambridge school' of historians of India (all initially based at the University of Cambridge). As one of the school's co-founders, Anil Seal, put it:

> Colonial systems of government, in which the alien few rule the native many, have tended to rely upon the support of some of their subjects, and the passivity of the majority; such a system is cheaper, and frequently less embarrassing. In India understandings between the Raj and some of its subjects

were a necessity if an off-shore island in north-western Europe was to govern hundreds of millions in South Asia. But these collaborations themselves varied both in their nature and in their intensity. Collaboration is a slippery term which may apply at any level between acquiescence and resignation. Men who worked with the foreign regime did so from a variety of motives: the wish to keep a position of importance or the hope of gaining such a position, the intention of working for an attractive regime or the habit of working for any regime, however unattractive. But in the physiology of colonialism it is results not motives that matter; and all those groups may be classed as collaborators whose actions fell in line with the purposes of the British. Such a system was not static, for yesterday's enemies might be tomorrow's allies. Neither was it uniform, because the unevenness of development throughout India called for different techniques in different regions.[38]

For Seal, the *raj* thus could not have functioned without Indian collaborators: bureaucrats, Western-educated literate elites, and rural notables who worked with and inside the colonial state. Crucially, this meant that 'an Indian role in the governance of the country' had endured after the British conquest. British rule built on, and did not entirely replace, earlier political and bureaucratic structures. **Collaboration** also set the limits to what the *raj* could attempt and achieve, if it was not to alienate those on whom it relied for its continued existence.[39]

This concept of **collaboration** was subsequently developed further by other historians of the Cambridge school. David Washbrook, for example, emphasized that the *raj* was able to extract the revenues it required from the peasants of Madras while deploying remarkably little coercive force. This was because Indian government servants were able to act as effective intermediaries between the *raj* and local notables, providing the British with the revenues that they required while allowing Indian rural leaders significant freedom to exert authority and power in local society. 'The whole system, and [the Indian official's] position within it, hinged on the fact that both sides sought an amicable compromise with as little fuss and interference as possible.'[40] All this was made possible by the fact that, for much of the nineteenth century, the British sought little more from their Indian subjects than revenues to pay for the Indian army. For the Cambridge school the *raj* meant continuity as much as change, in terms of who exercised the substance of power. Colonial rule involved the imposition of a thin veneer of British authority over long-established Indian structures of governance, a take-over rather than a demolition of indigenous regimes. Indians and Indian social structures fundamentally shaped the functioning of colonial governance. Indians remained active agents in the running and development of the state, and neither the coming of the British nor their subsequent sudden departure could be seen to mark a radical disjuncture in Indian history. This approach avowedly avoided the **Eurocentric** approach of some earlier imperial historians, giving Indians (rather than just British administrators) a key role as active agents in history and the running of the state. Yet it also implied that Indians had themselves played a major part in the maintenance and perpetuation of colonial rule. Some scholars deplore this interpretation as an attempt to shift the blame for 'colonialism' onto the shoulders of its victims, as will be discussed in Chapter 3.

The concept of **collaboration** was examined in the most systematic fashion, and extended far beyond India's shores, by Ronald Robinson. In many ways, it marked a natural continuation of Robinson and Gallagher's analysis of **informal empire**, indigenous state structures, and peripheral crises discussed in Chapter 1. Developing what Robinson called an 'excentric'[41] (as opposed to **Eurocentric**) theory of imperialism, emphasizing the role that forces and relationships on the **periphery** played in shaping empire, he argued that

> imperialism was as much a function of its victims' collaboration or non-collaboration – of their indigenous politics, as it was of European expansion. The expansive forces generated in industrial Europe had to combine with elements within the agrarian societies of the outer world to make empire at all practicable.[42]

In order for colonial rule to be both cheap and effective, local elites had to be recruited to help govern and had to be offered rewards for working in this capacity. The British could lend local elites assistance against their rivals at home and abroad, by providing access to wealth, technology, or military resources. If existing elites proved unreceptive, then the British might work with their enemies, overturn the status quo, and install new collaborators more amenable to British interests. But the British had to put resources into the relationship if it was to work, offering reasonably attractive terms and restraining the demands placed on non-European intermediaries.

Structures of **indirect rule** deployed by the British in parts of Africa could thus be seen as part of a much wider system of 'patron-client' relations and 'over-rule', subordinating but also preserving (or, indeed, actively creating) indigenous governing hierarchies.[43] This system was a response to practical requirements rather than a deeply thought-out and formalized general policy: the continuity of approach over almost two centuries is evidence of this. Theories of **collaboration** acknowledge that the British empire was not an all-powerful force, wiping the slate clean and building entirely new structures of exploitation and rule. Rather, colonial authority was reliant on key elements of non-European societies, and was limited in terms of how far and how fast it could move to change those inherited structures. To use a contemporary scholarly buzzword, empire almost inevitably involved hybridity, mixing heterogeneous and sometimes incongruous elements.

Robinson presented white settlers as the 'ideal prefabricated collaborators', pre-programmed with British ideas about enterprise, trade, and governance, and closely tied to British interests by their dependence upon the economic connection with 'home'. This is what made responsible self-government possible in the settler colonies. In Africa and Asia, Robinson argued, **collaboration** was always more difficult to achieve. Without formal imperial rule, it was hard to deliver the resources necessary to make stable collaborative bargains possible. The fruits of trade were too sparse, and could not be harvested quickly enough, to bolster the prestige of collaborating elites, who in turn seldom proved able to manage the integration of local economies into the world economic order. Almost everywhere (Japan was one exception), early collaborative bargains eventually collapsed along with local state structures. Subsequently, as the British established formal imperial control, they found new collaborators and struck new bargains. Under the aegis of colonial rule, they were able to provide these collaborators with the resources and authority to establish new state structures and new commercial relationships.

▶ Knowledge and colonial rule

With the 'cultural turn' in imperial history, some scholars have come to devote less attention to questions about the relationship between state structures and economic interests, or to analysing constitutional frameworks and the institutional apparatus of the colonial state. Instead, they have emphasized that empire was a 'cultural project', and that the control of colonial subjects was made possible by 'cultural technologies of rule'.[44] To some extent, this marks an extension of the concern among earlier generations of historians to understand how the flow of information (or, perhaps more accurately, the failure of information to flow) between **metropole** and colony influenced structures of control. But the new cultural turn goes much further than this, assigning the creation and control of knowledge a central place in the construction of concepts and structures of hierarchy and authority.

Here, scholars have followed the French theorist Michel Foucault in emphasizing that 'knowledge was both an effect and an instrument of power'.[45] They have also adopted Foucault's concept of governmentality: the idea that through pervasive forms of surveillance and classification, and through the control of information and knowledge, the state is able to exert power over the individual's body, identity, and sense of self. Power is enacted through institutions such as family structures, religion, organized sport, schools, clinics, prisons; through discourses of the human sciences, medicine, criminal justice, and demography; and through procedures which gather and control information including surveys, map-making, censuses, commissions of enquiry, statistical analysis, and the study and systematization of languages. If such structures work successfully, then individuals will eventually regulate their own behaviour in ways that further the state's ends. Little in the way of overt coercion is thus required.[46] Given what we have already seen about the connections between empire and state-building, and about debates concerning the degree to which the colonial state differed from the European nation-state, these ideas are of obvious interest to imperial historians.

When they have been applied to colonial rule, Foucault's ideas have often been refracted through Edward Said's arguments about 'Orientalism'. Said claimed that European Orientalists, supposed experts on Eastern politics, societies, and cultures, had in fact represented Asia in radically misleading ways. These errors were not innocent. Orientalism misinterpreted other societies in order to facilitate and justify their conquest. Colonial regimes subsequently sought to reshape their subjects to conform to the Orientalists' picture of what they should be like, and in the process make them easier to rule and exploit. Supposedly objective knowledge was thus in fact produced in such a way as to support unequal colonial power relations. Said argued that European writing about non-European societies, while disguised as neutral scientific description, in reality acted to establish the power of the colonial master over the indigenous subject.[47] These arguments have since been applied much more broadly to the history of the British and European empires.

Some scholars have thus argued for the existence and importance of what they have called colonial knowledge: 'the form and content of the knowledge that was produced out of and enabled resource exploitation, commerce, conquest, and colonization'.[48] Notably, it is claimed that the production of such knowledge involved a process of **othering**, emphasizing distinctions between European and non-European peoples, and indeed inventing such distinctions where none previously existed. This **othering** took place in order to mark and justify the unequal status of the colonizer and the colonized. Colonial knowledge 'created new categories and oppositions between colonizers and colonized, European and Asian, modern and traditional, West and East'.[49]

A parallel influence encouraging scholars to think about colonial knowledge and its role in representing and reshaping colonial societies came from the discipline of anthropology. Specifically, Bernard Cohn's work on colonial India emphasized the role played by the state in accumulating, shaping, and deploying knowledge in order to strengthen its own control over colonial subjects. Cohn directed attention towards the systematization of Indian languages by British officials, and towards the more general British drive to collect and use information and objects to facilitate rule. As Cohn put it, 'The conquest of India was a conquest of knowledge ... converting Indian forms of knowledge into European objects.'[50] Cohn, like Said, implied a radical break between the pre-colonial and colonial periods, the erasure of earlier forms of knowledge, and the creation of strikingly new structures under British rule.

Following this line of analysis, Nicholas Dirks has claimed that 'Colonialism was made possible, and then sustained and strengthened, *as much* by cultural technologies of rule as it was by the more obvious and brutal modes of conquest that first established power on foreign shores.'[51] However, many historians would object to the claim that cultural forces were *just as* important as economic or military power in building empires. Critics have also argued that the theories of Said, Cohn, and Dirks exaggerate the ability of Europeans to transform Asian and African societies, and leave colonial subjects without a role in their own history: they have 'sometimes served to marginalize Indians and their knowledge as thoroughly as the most hidebound colonial administrative history ever did'.[52]

There is a clear opposition here between theorists of colonial knowledge, and those who work with the concept of **collaboration**. Much of the resulting debate has been conducted in the arena provided by South Asian history. Criticism of Dirks and Cohn has been marked among those who share the Cambridge school's emphasis on the key role of Indian agents in British colonial rule. Thus much recent work by historians has stressed that the British *raj* did not just impose European knowledge and understandings of the East, but worked closely with various Indian collaborators to gather and harness Indian forms of knowledge. Indigenous groups could use their role in forming colonial knowledge to entrench their own privileged positions. Indian and British knowledge fused: again, hybridity is the watchword for much of this scholarship.[53]

Perhaps the most important and thought-provoking intervention in this debate has come from Christopher Bayly, in work that focuses on 'information' and 'intelligence' rather than colonial knowledge in accounting for British power in India. The *raj* was not, Bayly argues, based on misrepresentation and the imposition of European ideas, but rather on formidable and often successful attempts by the British to capture and utilize Indian sources of information. From the late eighteenth century, the British were able to recruit Indian running-spies, news-writers, and political secretaries, and thus out-compete Indian states in the war of intelligence. British understandings of India were based on continued engagement with Indian sources. This distorted Indian knowledge, but also gave Indian agents significant power in shaping their relationship with the British and opportunities to pursue their own interests. It was when Britain's control of Indian information networks failed, when the

British tried to impose their own military and civil, bureaucratic 'knowledge institutions' that the *raj* faced serious challenges to its authority. During the Mutiny and Rebellion of 1857, Indians turned 'modern' media of communication against the British, to organize and to communicate the message of revolt. Later, the Indian National Congress's campaigns against British rule were strengthened by a burgeoning Indian newspaper press and the remobilization of Indian information networks. British knowledge of India had clear limits, and the power it produced was never stable or all-encompassing. 'Information panics' showed the limits of the colonial state's control of information and intelligence. Whole areas of Indian life, vast networks of Indian social communication, remained beyond the ken of the colonial state.[54]

If theories of colonial knowledge have their limits for India, the case study from which they were derived in the first place, then almost inevitably their applicability to other areas is even more questionable. As Frederick Cooper has suggested, an emphasis on colonial knowledge offers little to advance our understanding of colonial rule in Africa, given the limited desire or ability of the colonial state there to intervene in local societies.[55] Similarly, in a study of British colonial officials in Africa in the first four decades of the twentieth century, Christopher Prior has argued that ideas about the role of colonial knowledge as the basis for power represent 'an attractive oversimplification'.[56] While some civilian officials might have sought to gather and create colonial knowledge to facilitate colonial rule, many of their military counterparts were far from convinced of the utility of such initiatives. The deployment of exemplary force, the protection of British prestige, and the use of spectacle, ceremony, and **invented tradition** remained a mainstay of the colonial state in Africa.

As we have already seen, historians need to factor the irrational into their understanding of British colonial rule, rather than assume that the colonial state simply worked to impose rational principles of bureaucratic governance. The colonial state certainly sought to gather knowledge about Africa and Africans, for instrumental purposes. But romantic, racialist notions about the 'unknowable' African remained. Some officials admired what they believed to be the 'traditional' features of African society, and sought neither to demystify nor to undermine them. Prior concludes that 'An ardent desire for knowledge was not an inherent product of the colonial encounter, but the result of a particular metropolitan mentality', one that was not shared by all colonial officials.[57]

▶ Conclusions

In the British empire, power was dispersed and authority devolved. Different colonies were governed in very different ways. Moreover, even when similar structures were built in different places, they often operated in significantly different ways. The reach of the colonial state down into Indian society was probably far less extensive in practice than in theory, and across tropical Africa it was even less formidable. If, as discussed in Chapter 1, the British empire can be seen as a mechanism for establishing strong state structures overseas to serve the requirements of British commerce and defence, then it clearly had its failures as well as successes. That the British dissolved their empire after the Second World War because its historic state-building mission had been accomplished seems unlikely: across Britain's Asian empire much of that work still seemed incomplete, and in Africa it had only just begun.

Even in Britain's settler colonies, the imperial and colonial authorities did not create structures of governance that were exact duplicates of those established in Britain. Indeed, such structures varied considerably within the United Kingdom itself: most notably, Ireland was governed very differently than England, Scotland, or Wales. The gap separating practices of governance in Britain and its colonies in tropical Africa and Asia was even greater. Nevertheless, as we have seen, there were borrowings in both directions. During the nineteenth and twentieth centuries, those in control of Europe's colonies often saw the nation-state, as embodied in the practices of their home country, as the ideal form of governance. During this period nation-states seemed to be emerging and becoming stronger both within and beyond Europe's borders. Colonial administrators could not help but be influenced by their understandings of 'the norms, inventions, and processes of the apparently successful nation-state' at home.[58] They also brought ideas from the colonies back to Britain and Europe, which in turn influenced thinking about governance in the metropole.

We should thus refrain from treating the histories of the colonial state and the European nation-state as entirely separate. Indeed, some of the underlying questions that historians ask about the two are essentially the same. In both cases, scholars debate the role played by government in supporting and protecting different economic and social interest groups, and disagree as to whether the state is best understood as an essentially neutral mediator in social conflict or as the tool of dominant elites. We should also acknowledge that if the colonial state was extremely varied in the forms that it took, then so too was the European nation-state. Rather than propose a simple model of binary opposition between colonial state and nation-state, it is probably more helpful to visualize a spectrum of state forms and structures, and to allow for a considerable degree of overlap between metropolitan and colonial approaches to governance.

Yet, if we set the case of the self-governing settler colonies to one side, then the colonial state surely does seem different from the European nation-state in at least one fundamental respect. Although British colonial administrators claimed to be fulfilling a humanitarian duty towards colonial subjects, discharging their role as trustees, the ultimate loyalties of those administrators were owed to the metropolitan **core** territory.[59] Britain's colonial states might have been free from day-to-day supervision by London, but in the last resort they were answerable to London, and were staffed at senior levels by British people whose own first duty was to Britain and British interests. This became most clearly apparent at moments of dire need. Extremely limited responses to massive famine mortality in Ireland (1845–52) and in Bengal (1943) arguably offered stark proof of the priorities of the colonial state.[60]

Moreover, colonial states did not grant all their subjects full political rights, and often provided for separate economic and political treatment on the basis of perceived racial difference. Some European states did this too, but colonial states (unlike their European counterparts) did little to promote a sense of overarching, unifying national identity among their subjects. Until the very last years of empire in Asia and Africa, British colonial administrators seldom sought to legitimate their rule by appealing to national unity. Indeed, some have argued that colonial states engaged actively in policies of 'divide and rule', seeking to separate out different groups of colonial subjects and turn them against one another, in order to reduce the threat of opposition. Whether this is true or not, when colonial states in Africa sought rapid economic and social change after the Second World War, they found that their attempts to encourage colonial economic development were undermined by the 'absence of a single moral community'.[61] Some would argue that this lack of a history of nation-building also had profoundly damaging consequences for African states after they became independent of British rule. The next chapter engages with these issues at close quarters, examining theories about how the British empire managed, strengthened, and even created difference among its subject peoples.

3 Difference

▶ **A world-shaping force?**

Did the British empire fundamentally reshape existing economic, political, social, and cultural structures and patterns in the colonies? If so, how, and to what ends? Did overseas expansion transform Britain itself? Was the contemporary belief that the British empire could be a 'world-shaping force' justified?[1] Or did empire generally work to preserve and perpetuate pre-existing ways of organizing and governing society in Britain and its colonies? In assessing the usefulness of the various theories and concepts that purport to explain the economic and strategic purposes of imperial expansion and the nature of the colonial state, historians have often been obliged to consider the potentially transformative effects of empire. As we have seen in the previous two chapters, in doing so they have often adopted markedly divergent positions.

As we have also seen, historians have moved beyond simple models that seek to attribute the imperial expansionist drive to any one particular group in British society. Instead, many now accept pluralist accounts of imperial expansion and colonial rule. Commercial and financial elites did not oblige British governments to expand, and were not able to turn colonial states into straightforward tools of economic exploitation. British empire-building was driven by broad geopolitical and economic goals, serving worldwide strategic ends rather than seeking to secure opportunities for particular commercial interest groups. Moreover, outside the settler colonies and key trading outposts, in Asia and particularly in Africa the colonial states set up around the British empire were often far less formidable and interventionist than has sometimes been assumed. All this means that, if we want to understand the forces encouraging social, cultural, economic, and political transformation in Britain and its colonies, we need to move beyond a narrow focus on commercial lobbyists, gentlemanly capitalists, politicians, policy-makers, or the colonial state. We need to broaden our frame of analysis to include a range of non-official European agents who were also kept busy by the work of empire: entrepreneurs, settlers, missionaries, social reformers, and so forth. Crucially, we also need to examine the roles played by a wide range of non-European agents in shaping power relations in the colonies and across the empire.

Yet making this leap into pluralism inevitably brings us into conceptually difficult territory. It is one thing to group the actions of the imperial and colonial states, and the consequences of imperial and colonial governance, together under the label 'empire'. It is another matter to aggregate the work of all the different Europeans who were operating in territories of **formal** and **informal empire**, all the varied intentions behind and consequences of their actions, and their sometimes tenuous connections with the authority of imperial or colonial governments, and label this 'empire' also. Governments were not always willing or able to control aggressive settlers waging an undeclared frontier war against indigenous peoples, or missionaries operating well beyond the boundaries of formal colonial territory, or traders selling guns, alcohol, or opium. Moreover, modern British imperial expansion was occurring at the same time as a whole range of other new technologies seemed also to be transforming relationships between widely separated parts of the world: steamships and railways; telegraphs; mass production; the mass media; rapid-fire and accurate small arms and artillery. What elements of this complex, chaotic, and at times toxic mixture should we label as 'empire'? Do we restrict our analysis to those aspects which demonstrate a clear connection with formal political power, with the imperial and colonial states? Or should we think in terms of an all-encompassing 'colonialism' which covers virtually every aspect of 'modernity' and its impact on the globe? And do we also need to think about some counterfactuals? After all, even if European states had engaged in neither formal territorial annexation nor the exercise of informal imperial influence, then European agents might still have entered into similarly unequal economic and cultural relationships, at similar times, and in similar places beyond Europe's boundaries. How do we separate out the coercive from the consensual elements of the European overseas presence? At what point did consensual European engagement with other places end, and empire begin? To complicate matters further, the actions of some British individuals and groups operating within territories of formal and informal empire may have gone directly against the expressed wishes and interests of the British imperial and colonial states. Missionaries, who entered into an extremely ambiguous relationship with government policy-makers, might be considered as the key example here.[2] How much power, then, do concepts of 'empire' or 'colonialism' hold as analytical tools, once we move beyond the conveniently well-defined sphere of the state?

In order to explore these problems, this chapter moves into the realm of cultural history, and focuses on the role of the British empire in creating and perpetuating difference. This issue has been at the heart of much recent historical writing, which has drawn on and contested a range of theoretical influences and has generated an extensive historiographical debate.

As discussed in Chapter 2, many historians argue that colonial states displayed an active drive to divide their subjects, in order to rule them more effectively. This involved emphasizing the differences that marked out various groups of subjects by creating, strengthening, or systematizing ideas about race, class, caste, and gender. Colonial states 'dealt in heterogeneity by naturalising ethnic difference and essentialising racial inequality'.[3] They encouraged rulers, administrators, and subjects to imagine the existence of fundamental divisions within colonial societies, in order to build and justify inequalities and hierarchies. Colonial rule also, it is claimed, involved emphasizing and sometimes legislating for a fundamental difference between white rulers and non-white subjects. Partha Chatterjee has argued that the most basic premise of the colonial state was 'the rule of colonial difference, namely, the preservation of the alienness of the ruling group'.[4] Colonial rulers had to seem different from and superior to their subjects, in order to pull off the tricks of the trades of dominance and governance.

We have already encountered the argument that the colonial state ruled in a distinctive fashion, compared to the European nation-state. Jane Burbank and Frederick Cooper draw a broader distinction between empires and nation-states, arguing that

> Empires are large political units ... polities that maintain distinction and hierarchy as they incorporate new people. The nation-state, in contrast, is based on the idea of a single people in a single territory constituting itself as a unique political community ... The concept of empire presumes that different peoples within the polity will be governed differently.

According to this definition, the maintenance (and perhaps the creation) of difference is fundamental to what an empire is.[5]

Histories which emphasize the role played by colonial rule in creating or intensifying difference share many of the same theoretical underpinnings as the work on colonial knowledge discussed in Chapter 2 above. As well as adopting perspectives from the discipline of anthropology, these accounts have borrowed the concept of **othering** from literary and cultural theory. This concept suggests that when people define who they are, they do so in opposition to an 'other' which they see as their direct opposite. The concept of **othering** also suggests that, perhaps paradoxically, people establish a range of intimate connections with the 'other' against which they are defining themselves. Colonial rule, it is thus argued, meant that British people defined themselves against subject peoples, who were their 'other', but in the process also created connections with colonial subjects that formed an essential part of their own identities. Colonialism brought 'the effect of seeming to exclude the other absolutely from the self, in a world divided absolutely into two ... What is overlooked, in producing this modern effect of order, is the dependence of such identity upon what it excludes.'[6] Such claims form the basis for one of the key arguments of the **new imperial history**: that British and colonial identities were 'mutually constitutive' of one another, and that British identity was decisively influenced by the imperial experience.

Yet despite these accounts, many historians are not convinced that the British empire fully lived up to its image as a world-shaping force, or that it played a consistently transformative role through the creation of difference. Just as they have doubted the ability of the colonial state fundamentally to re-shape local economies and societies, so some scholars have maintained that the cultural impact of colonial rule was in many cases limited. Susan Bayly thus argues, for instance, that

> Despite its apparent capacity to reshape minds as well as material environments in the age of the steam-powered loom, the railway, and the Gatling gun, coloni-alism was far from being an all-powerful agent of change in any extra-European society. Even where British power was exercised most intrusively, both through the use of military force and in the great Victorian enterprise of scientific data-collection, much of the colonial world was only lightly and unevenly touched by Western-style schools, laws, printing presses, and campaigns of missionary evangelism.[7]

If this was the case, then was the British empire really able to create or inten-sify difference, in a transformative fashion? This chapter presents and analyses different perspectives on this question. First, it looks at historical writing about India, further examining the ideas of both the Cambridge school of South Asian history and the rather different Subaltern Studies school. It then moves on to consider writing about the British empire and race more generally, looking at how ideas about racial difference took shape in different colonies, and at what political, social, and cultural effects those ideas had. This topic intersects with scholarship on gender divisions, and the chapter concludes by considering the impact of feminist theories and perspectives on the writing of the history of the British empire.

▶ Difference and the Indian *raj*

Historians of India have debated the transformative potential of British impe-rial rule with particular intensity. Some have presented the colonial state as a formidable, intrusive influence, reshaping South Asia's economy, politics, societies, and cultures. Others have depicted the *raj* as a strictly limited presence, with neither the desire nor the resources to transform India. At the most, these historians argue, British rule reinforced existing tendencies in Indian life: it always remained dependent upon the **collaboration** of the Indian elite. Indeed, the concept of **collaboration** is central to these debates. As we saw in Chapter 2, from the late 1960s the Cambridge school challenged the idea that British rule was an alien, entirely authoritarian imposition on Indian society. Rather, the *raj* applied but a thin veneer of British authority to existing Indian governmental and social structures. The British merely sought to extract from India the revenues necessary to support the Indian army, the key tool of British power in Asia. They were able to do this by working with Indian collaborators: Indian government servants and cooperative rural notables. Arising from this basic model is the argument that the British had neither the wish nor the ability to transform Indian society, and that ideas about racial difference were at best peripheral, and at worst detrimental, to the crucial mechanisms of **collaboration**. According to this view, the 'rule of colonial difference' was not fundamental to colonial governance, but was one of the things that ultimately undermined it as superior British racial attitudes obstructed the effective functioning of the colonial state. David Washbrook thus argues that if the British helped shape Indian society, then they did so by reinforcing existing Indian patterns and tendencies. British rule restructured South Asian society and economy in ways that strengthened 'tradition', or at least what was perceived to be customary and traditional in Indian society. The colonial state thus encouraged the 'peasantization' of Indian society and stripped the dynamism out of other sectors of the economy. Literacy and urbanization declined, and mobility was reduced as society was 'sedentarized' and tied to the land. However, these processes did not prevent Indian commercial elites from prospering in the big cities. British rule 'put the possessors of capital, whatever their ethnic origins, into an increasingly dominant and privileged position over producers and labourers'.[8]

A very different take on the transformative effects of the *raj* has been offered by those influenced by insights from the discipline of anthropology, and particularly by the work of Bernard Cohn. Nicholas Dirks has taken up and developed Cohn's ideas about the impact of colonial rule, discussed above in Chapter 2. Dirks argues that India's modern caste system is not 'some unchanged survival of ancient India' but rather 'the product of an historical encounter between India and Western colonial rule'. Dirks does not claim that caste was simply invented by the British to make India easier to rule and to promote British interests. Nevertheless, he holds that the idea of caste was developed and systematized under British rule in such a way as to make it a

66 British Imperial History

more powerful means for enshrining division within Indian society. For Dirks, 'colonialism made caste what it is today', even if it was Indians who themselves indulged in 'Orientalist nostalgia' as they did the work of thinking and writing about, and systematizing, caste.[9] This, after all, is supposedly one of the sources of the power of Orientalism: that the colonized end up believing what the colonizer says about them.

Dirks is also fiercely critical of the work of the Cambridge school. He denies that Indian elites seized on British rule as a means to further their own interests, and that they only turned against the colonial state when it ceased to provide the power and influence that they required. He argues that the concept of **collaboration** is a mere device which allows historians to ignore the oppressive and violent nature of British colonial rule, and to downplay the forcefulness and legitimacy of Indian nationalism. 'The salience of the historical structures of colonial rule cannot be trivialized by pointing to a handful of Indian "capitalists" who managed to secure wealth for themselves during colonial times.'[10]

Partha Chatterjee similarly sees the arguments of the Cambridge school as a means of 'turning the tables', of relieving the British of responsibility for Indian economic or social problems and instead blaming Indians for their own subordination and poverty. The Cambridge school, Chatterjee argues, presents colonialism and 'colonial underdevelopment' as the products of 'indigenous history'.

> There is something magical about a 'historical theory' that can with such ease spirit away the violent intrusion of colonialism and make all of its features the innate property of an indigenous history ... Like all feats of magic, however, this achievement of 'historical theory' is also an illusion.[11]

Those who have been targeted for criticism by Dirks and Chatterjee have responded in equally vigorous terms. As we have seen, Christopher Bayly has emphasized the role of Indian agents and Indian information and intelligence in supporting British colonial rule. He has also argued, more broadly, that accounts that emphasize the 'rule of colonial difference' and the transformative effects of colonial rule are simply unable convincingly to explain the enduring nature of colonial states that could call on only tiny numbers of white officials.

> India's alienness could never be too crudely asserted by a government dependent on an army of Indian subordinate servants. It was difficult to sustain an 'apartheid' ideology stressing ineluctable racial difference in a subcontinent where Indians continued to control – albeit under severe constraint – the vast

bulk of capital and almost the whole means of agricultural production. Colonial officials, missionaries and businessmen were forced to register the voices of native informants in ideology and heed them in practice even if they despised and misrepresented them.[12]

Similar, in directly refuting Dirks' arguments, Susan Bayly claims that caste was not the figment of an Orientalist imagination, but reflected a deeply rooted set of Indian social practices. Profound continuities existed between understandings of caste in the pre-colonial and colonial eras, and while changes did occur, these did not necessarily reflect conscious manipulation intended to facilitate colonial rule. Indians played the key role in the processes by which understandings of caste shifted over time.[13] For John Darwin, all this makes it unlikely that British officials had the power to transform South Asian identities and culture in order to facilitate colonial rule.

It was always more likely that the encoding of custom and the ascribing of status were cooperative ventures. Their terms were bound to derive from well-placed informants with a great deal at stake. No doubt, the authorised versions were drafted to help the loyal collaborator and shore up his claims. But they could hardly ignore the 'local knowledge' of oral tradition or, in literate societies, the opinion of scholars and scribes. It followed from this that the forms of ethnic identity, whether tribal or caste-like, were the product not so much of Machiavellian repression as of pragmatic reciprocity.[14]

▶ **Subaltern Studies**

A rather different approach to the history of colonial India has been offered by members of the Subaltern Studies school. These scholars did not deny the central arguments of the Cambridge school about **collaboration** between the colonial state and the Indian elite. Indeed, in a way, they accepted them as a given, and argued that historians should as a result discount earlier, nationalist Indian historical writing which saw the elite as the champions of national interests in a liberation struggle against British rule. But rather than focus on the mechanisms of **collaboration**, Subaltern Studies urged historians to move away from examining the political elite altogether, and instead to write histories that were about neither colonial rule nor the nationalist narrative. In its early years at least (before turning towards postcolonial modes of theoretical analysis in the 1980s) Subaltern Studies sought to recover the history of those excluded from such narratives, scouring the archives and using the methods of oral history to uncover traces that might allow us to write the history of the peasant masses in their own terms.

Subaltern Studies was in part a response to E. P. Thompson's call to write 'history from below'.[15] It also drew on the ideas of the Italian Marxist Antonio Gramsci. Gramsci had sought to explain how dominant groups used culture to perpetuate their control over society and the economy – how they exerted what Gramsci called **hegemony** – and how subordinate classes or **subalterns** could overturn that **hegemony**. For Gramsci, consensus was not a sign of the existence of a fundamentally egalitarian order in which all benefited equally from the way that state and society were structured. Rather, consensus could occur despite major social, economic, and political inequalities, because the subordinated had been persuaded to identify with the hegemonic order of things. As Raymond Williams put it,

> Hegemony is then not only the articulate upper level of 'ideology', nor are its forms of control only those ordinarily seen as 'manipulation' or 'indoctrination'. It is the whole body of practice and expectations, over the whole of living: our senses and assignments of energy, our shaping perceptions of ourselves and our world. It is a lived system of meanings and values … It thus constitutes a sense of reality for most people in the society.[16]

Subaltern Studies drew on these ideas about **hegemony** as part of an attempt to question the established pieties of nationalist historiography, to undermine the narrative that pitted Indian elites, as bearers of objective national interests, against British overlords. This narrative not only focused overwhelmingly on elites, but also (and perhaps purposely) ignored the extent to which those elites had failed to pursue the interests of the peasant masses before or after independence. Ranajit Guha thus criticized a dominant Indian nationalist way of writing history that worked to

> uphold Indian nationalism as a phenomenal expression of the goodness of the native elite with the antagonistic aspect of their relation to the colonial regime made, against all evidence, to look larger than its collaborationist aspect, their role as promoters of the cause of the people than that as exploiters and oppressors, their altruism and self-abnegation than their scramble for the modicum of power and privilege granted by the rulers in order to make sure of their support for the Raj. The history of Indian nationalism is thus written up as a sort of spiritual biography of the Indian elite.[17]

Guha emphasized that the mass of the Indian people in fact lived in a largely autonomous realm, outside elite **hegemony**, and that the elites never tried to lead peasant resistance against the British in a genuinely national liberation movement. To have done so would have posed too great a risk to their own privileged status. Guha urged scholars to recover an historical sense of peasant culture, of peasant interests separate from and generally in opposition to those of local Indian elites. Episodes of peasant rebellion could, it was claimed, offer useful entry points. At such moments autonomous peasant thinking and agendas were revealed with unusual clarity and (thanks to the need to repress such rebellions) recorded in detail by those in power.[18]

Subaltern Studies emphasized that peasants had **agency**, and were not passive victims of oppression by British and Indian elites. Although subordinated, peasants retained some power to influence their own destinies, and historians as a result needed to understand 'the distinctive idioms of peasant protest – its religious and communitarian language and its ability to appropriate but also subvert elite political practice'. However, Jon Wilson has suggested that this is an overly simplistic approach. For Wilson, power is produced through the interaction of different people and groups, in relationships that change over time, and is not simply held (or not held) by individuals. To understand power in colonial India, we thus need to examine the interactions between the colonial state and Indians at all levels of society.[19]

▶ Colonialism and race

Historians of the British empire in India have thus debated at some length whether and how the colonial state perpetuated and created differences of status, caste, and race in order to facilitate colonial rule. Similar questions have preoccupied some historians of other parts of Asia, and of Africa.

Some have focused on the role of the colonial state in transforming hierarchies of power within African societies. Terence Ranger for example examined how, in devising ways to govern Africans more effectively, colonial rulers reshaped African society. Superficially, British colonial officials emphasized that they were ruling Africa through 'traditional' mechanisms, working through African tribal structures and leaders. However, Ranger argued that African societies typically did not possess the fixed structures and hierarchies required by the British to rule: they were more fluid and dynamic than this. Colonial officials thus **invented tradition**, creating suitable structures to facilitate rule, imposing and strengthening the categories of tribal and ethnic identities, creating and formalizing hierarchies, bolstering the fragile authority of tribal elders, and thus 'transforming flexible custom into hard prescription'.[20]

While Ranger examined status distinctions within African societies, many other historians have focused on the creation of hierarchies of race, and on perceptions of racial difference. They have tended to argue that ideas about racial difference were both a product of imperial conquest and colonial rule and a means of strengthening and perpetuating British authority in the colonies. Drawing on Gramsci's theories, they have also sometimes argued or implied that ideas about race operated as a hegemonic ideology, both in Britain and in the colonies.

Yet the picture is not as clear as these simple, basic points might lead us to believe. Victorian and Edwardian definitions of 'race' were complex and confused. They incorporated both a belief in essential and immutable biological differences between different peoples, and a sense that race involved cultural characteristics that were amenable to change.[21] While some contemporaries argued that non-whites were inherently inferior, and that continued colonial rule, segregation, and 'separate development' were thus justified, others claimed that different peoples could be 'assimilated' into British cultural, social, political, and economic structures. Nineteenth-century scientific research and discourse did less to resolve this debate in favour of biological theories of immutable difference than some historians have claimed. Both segregationist and assimilationist ways of thinking were 'racist', but the practical outcomes in terms of legal and legislative structures were very different.[22]

Moreover, we also need to bear in mind that the extension and maintenance of British imperial authority did not inevitably depend on the exaggeration of racial difference. For example, while Christopher Bayly acknowledges that British expansion in the late-eighteenth and early-nineteenth century was supported by a strong sense of national identity, he denies that this was primarily based on ideas about racial difference. For Bayly, Britain's aristocracy believed in the excellence of their religion, science, and institutions. They sought to spread what they saw as a benevolent new order, tolerant of diverse traditions and beliefs. They were thus able to 'appease and integrate the huge variety of native leaders and soldiers who served in the imperial armies'. In India and North America, British officers happily 'went native', adopting local practices and dress, and entering into relationships with indigenous women, rendering British imperial power even more formidable.[23] Few would go as far as David Cannadine and argue that, across the sweep of its nineteenth- and twentieth-century history, the British empire was primarily a means of replicating and maintaining divisions of class rather than race.[24] Nevertheless, it would be misleading to claim that ideas about racial difference were monolithic and unchanging, or that they had simple and uniform effects across the British empire.

Following the abolition of slavery in 1834, some humanitarians and policymakers claimed that the British empire was, or should be, 'colour-blind'. British subjects, regardless of skin colour or other external markers of difference, could and should enjoy the same political rights. Yet, in practice, race acted as a significant determinant of political and social rights and of economic opportunities, and in the late nineteenth century the idea of a colour-blind empire lost much of its potency in British political debates. Colonial administrators were therefore to some extent able to use race as an organizing principle, the basis for policies of 'divide and rule' that kept colonial populations disunited and thus made them easier to govern. Nevertheless, it would be wrong to argue that colonial rule was based on a simple division between whites and non-whites, or that modes of governance were determined purely by ideas about race. Ethnic, linguistic, and religious differences represented problems as well as opportunities for colonial rulers, who might thus attempt to minimize rather than exaggerate their significance.[25] Empire might have shaped British (and non-British) attitudes towards race, and *vice versa*, but those relation-ships were complex. Hierarchies were not always structured along strictly racial lines. Different groups experienced empire in very different ways, according to highly varied local circumstances.

For many of Britain's black colonial subjects, empire meant increased local or global mobility, and exposure to new cultural influences coming from differ-ent parts of Africa, from Britain, and from elsewhere. Africans were not always able to choose whether to embrace this new cultural hybridity. Enslavement and plantation life were powerful motors of forced cultural change, involv-ing transportation across the Atlantic to the West Indies. In Britain's slave colonies, black political and economic rights were non-existent or severely restricted, and black communities were divided and disrupted. Slavery shaped demographics, having a significant impact on mortality, fertility, and family structures. Sexual intercourse (often non-consensual) between white men and black women also created a significant and growing body of 'free people of colour', people of mixed race who demanded political rights. Slavery also contributed to the mixing of linguistic, musical, religious, and other cultural forms. In the second half of the twentieth century, migration from the West Indies to Britain in search of work meant that Britain itself became a significant place where inequality was experienced, connections among nationalists could be developed, and black experiences of empire were forged. For those who expe-rienced colonial rule in Africa during the nineteenth and twentieth centuries, unequal treatment and racial policies of exclusion could meanwhile reinforce senses of tribal, national, or pan-African identity.[26]

Empire also shaped British thinking about race and racial difference. Slavery played a particularly important role in this regard, linking skin col-our with ideas about the inferiority and superiority of different groups. Counterintuitively, the campaigns to abolish the slave trade and slavery may have further contributed to this way of thinking, reinforcing popular British associations between blacks and passivity, poverty, and subordination. Even after the abolition of slavery, the West Indies continued to loom large in British thinking about race. Once the legal support for white supremacy provided by slavery disappeared, a defensive white racism became more coherent and aggressive. The economic decline of the West Indies also created new tensions. Former slaves refused to work on the plantations, instead moving into subsistence and small-scale farming activities of their own on inferior land. Britain's move away from protectionism and towards free trade meanwhile robbed sugar producers of their privileged access to British markets, and left them exposed to competition from cheap, slave-produced sugar shipped from other parts of the Caribbean. In the resulting debate about the economic stagnation of the islands, some argued that blacks were lazy and unsuited to the responsibilities of economic and political liberty, and that the abolition of slavery had caused the economic collapse.[27] For some commentators, the Morant Bay rising in Jamaica in 1865 offered further evidence that racial difference was biological and insurmountable, and that blacks were irredeemably inferior to whites. Along with the Indian Mutiny of 1857 and the continuing military conflict with Maori in New Zealand, Morant Bay contributed to a mid-century hardening of racial attitudes.[28] Yet for other contemporaries, the rising could be bound into a wider critique of inequality that transcended perceived racial divisions. Black freedmen in Jamaica and white workers in Britain were all engaged in the same struggle to defend their liberties and defeat unjust and oppressive regimes.[29] Divisions of race and class intersected in complex ways, and were not necessarily mutually reinforcing.

Compared with the West Indies, Africa may have played a less powerful role in shaping British thinking about race. This reflected the fact that British engagement with Africa was limited in its nature and extent until late in the nineteenth century, and was relatively short-lived. For much of the nineteenth century, British authority in Africa was restricted to small coastal enclaves, and was heavily dependent on the goodwill and support of local African leaders. This meant that economic, political, and cultural relations were complex and reciprocal, and were not characterized by out-and-out British domination. Isolated British representatives were hardly in control of the situation on the ground, and depended on Africans for knowledge of the land and its peoples. Outcomes remained unpredictable and resistance could be significant. Often operating beyond the reach of the colonial state, missionaries and entrepreneurs strengthened and widened the British presence, but (outside southern Africa) were seldom a formidable force.[30] If we accept the argument (presented in Chapter 1) that the Scramble for Africa was not driven primarily by commercial interests, then it follows that much of British expansion in the late nineteenth century lacked any clear economic motive and was not accompanied by a strong sense of how new colonies could be governed and made profitable. Africans were thus able to retain a significant, if limited, degree of autonomy. **Indirect rule** confirmed the authority of 'traditional' African leaders, and even the 'second colonial invasion' and economic development drive that followed the Second World War had but a limited impact on much of African society.

Empire thus did not shape British thinking about race in a clear and straight-forward fashion. Assigning 'colonialism' an overwhelming significance in this regard, as in so many others, can lead us to ignore important variations between places and periods, and to neglect the non-imperial influences that worked on Britain and its colonies. Focusing on discourses about race and intermarriage, Damon Salesa has for example argued that 'racial crossing' was sometimes seen by Victorians as a cause for alarm, but at other times as a means to resolve conflict and overcome resistance. Racial crossing could strengthen colonial rule and bridge the divide between settlers and indigenous peoples. 'At different moments in different places, racial crossing meant widely variant, even contradictory things.'[31]

In terms of how racial differences were understood, and how those under-standings translated into action, there could be a particularly significant diver-gence between those in the metropole and those working 'on the spot'. In the colonies, 'agents of empire and the subjects of colonial rule negotiated a bal-ance of coercion and consent that differed according to the contexts of place and time in each locality … [As a result] metropolitan values and imperial practices often stood in contradiction to one another.'[32] Divergences between policy-makers in London and white settlers on the frontiers of Britain's empire could be particularly marked, although the imperial state often found it neither practical nor desirable forcefully to impose its will on colonists as they went about the violent dispossession of indigenous peoples or the exclusion of non-white migrants.

Racial difference did not inevitably mean segregation and the exclusion of non-Europeans from positions of power: if it had, then mechanisms of **collaboration** would simply have broken down. In port settlements such as Freetown (Sierra Leone), Lagos (Nigeria), and Cape Town (South Africa), African creoles occupied privileged positions, engaged in the administration of colo-nial government and the running of the local economy. Many of these creoles saw themselves as 'black Englishmen', buying into British forms of education and socialization, and enjoying (or at least claiming) the same social and polit-ical status as whites. Increasingly, however, whites denied their right to do so. Ideas about 'separate development' gained greater currency during the closing decades of the nineteenth century, both in Britain and among settlers, expatri-ates, and administrators in the colonies. Whites began to spurn creoles as inau-thentic 'mimic men', neither properly British nor properly African, and thus inferior and unreliable. The economic, social, and political status of creoles suffered as a result.[33] Nevertheless, in South Africa people of mixed race still managed to 'escape the worst of British and settler racism by claiming to be different – to be Coloured rather than "Bantu"'.[34] In West Africa, creoles continued to play significant economic and administrative roles throughout the twentieth century.

► Gender and empire

We can also explore the theme of difference by looking at the recent work of feminist historians of empire, who have played a particularly prominent role in writing the **new imperial history**. Deploying diverse theories and concepts, drawn from a range of fields, these scholars have sought to prove that almost every aspect of the history of the British empire was 'gendered'. Angela Woollacott thus argues that gender was 'one of the forces driving and shaping the empire' and also 'a set of ideologies produced at once in the colonies and the metropole that constituted shifting and pervasive imperial culture'. Woollacott sees gender as an all-pervasive force:

> British historians must recognize gender as a foundational dynamic that shaped all aspects of the empire from the conduct of war, to the drafting of statutes and regulations, to social and medical codes governing sexuality, to stories that appeared variously in *The Times* and in juvenile fiction. Ideas of gender, always linked to 'race' and class, were forged in the colonies as well as in the metropole and circulated constantly throughout the empire.[35]

This claim that gender inequalities interacted with, and often reinforced, racial and class hierarchies is central to much feminist writing on the history of empire. Gender, race, and class worked in relation to one another perhaps most obviously in the slave plantations of the eighteenth- and early-nineteenth-century British West Indies. Male and female whites exerted power over blacks of both genders. However, wealthy white male plantation owners were able to exert various forms of authority over other white males and females, as well as over black slaves. Meanwhile, black men might exert authority over other black men, as overseers, and over black women, at home as well as in the workplace. White males might supplement marital sex with white females with sex with black slaves, very often through coercion. Sexual unions between white men and black women (unions between black men and white women were not tolerated in the same way, and were far less frequent) produced people of mixed race, who could be enslaved or free, and who were indeed sometimes adopted by their white fathers and raised to a privileged socio-economic position. The private and public politics of these densely interwoven networks of inequality were always fraught.[36]

Recent historical writing on gender and empire has also been marked by an awareness of the **Eurocentric** nature of earlier feminist work. Earlier feminists often failed to consider the particularities of the experience of African and Asian women, and tended to impose European patterns, norms, and ideals on non-European places and people.[37] Newer scholarship has, in contrast, examined the role of white women as agents of the colonial state and of imperial power, as humanitarians and as 'imperialists'.

From an early stage, white British women played a voluntary role in various political campaigns relating to the empire. Clare Midgley has explored the role played by middle-class women and women's associations in British popular mobilization against the slave trade and slavery during the late eighteenth and early nineteenth centuries. Women helped shape the nature of these campaigns, particularly at a provincial level, and brought different concerns and skills to the task than did male participants. This helped them generate broader popular support for the cause. However, as Midgley emphasizes, few women treated their involvement in these campaigns as a chance to overturn established barriers to female involvement in politics. Reflecting the nature of the wider movement, women's anti-slavery campaigning was framed as philanthropy rather than as a political campaign linked to black resistance or working-class agitation for greater rights at home. Midgley thus shows how women's involvement in the anti-slavery campaigns was very much a product of its time, conditioned by established hierarchies of class and gender, conventional beliefs about Britain's imperial mission and Evangelical Christianity, and the combination of 'a belief in black humanity with a conviction of African cultural inferiority'.[38]

Antoinette Burton has similarly looked at imperial influences on and contexts for the British feminist movement in the late nineteenth and early twentieth centuries. She presents India in particular as a key point of reference for British feminists in this period.[39] Lisa Chilton has meanwhile examined the role played by women's voluntary societies in generating and shaping flows of female migrants from Britain to Canada and Australia. These societies worked to make emigration safer and to exclude the 'unsuitable'. Such activities provided a sphere in which women could exercise and increase their social and political power, and help shape ideas about imperial and settler society. They also reflected and helped determine hierarchies of status in settler societies: indigenous and non-British women were marginalized in these associations.[40]

White women also played a significant role in the 'second colonial invasion' that followed the Second World War. In this period, British policy-makers sought to promote rapid economic development in Africa, to provide the food and raw materials that would support Britain's post-war economic recovery. This involved increasing the size and scope of the colonial state, and adopting more interventionist policies aimed at reshaping African lives and economic activities. As small numbers of British women began to gain access to the world of academia, and to the health and welfare professions (which became 'feminized' after the Second World War), so they played a prominent part in the development and implementation of colonial development policies. Yet this did not necessarily mean that the role of African women was better understood or more effectively built into post-war development policies.[41]

The colonial state and non-official British interests and lobby groups sometimes worked to intervene in and transform gender relations in Britain's colonies. Historical work on this issue has been informed by a range of theoretical influences, including the ideas about governmentality discussed in Chapter 2. Philippa Levine has for example examined the regulation of prostitution in the British empire and the impact of such legislation on women in the colonies. Regulations were primarily aimed at restricting the spread of venereal disease among British soldiers stationed overseas. However, it was the prostitutes (rather than the soldiers) who were held responsible for the spread of disease, and who were thus closely regulated and inspected and sometimes imprisoned. Levine looks at a range of policies deployed in a number of colonies, and how these shifted over time. The net result, she argues, was the creation of new state powers to intrude into the lives of women, increased gender inequality, and increased resistance. Thinking about venereal disease became linked with concepts of civilization, race, class, and gender.[42]

Meanwhile, improving the status of women, or at least making the status of women conform to British ideas of what was right and proper, was sometimes seen as part of Britain's 'civilizing mission' and task of trusteeship. The nineteenth-century campaign against the Indian practice of *suttee* (widow-burning) was framed in terms of improving not just the status of women but Indian society more generally. The campaigners succeeded in convincing the colonial state to intervene against the practice.[43] Elsewhere, in the Pacific Islands for example, campaigners targeted social practices that, by British standards, seemed to give women too much independence.

During the twentieth century, colonial rule in tropical Africa involved attempts by missionaries as well as by colonial officials to regulate the lives of women. To a degree this involved the imposition of British norms and thinking about gender relations and sexuality, as part of a broader attempt to introduce 'order' and 'civilization'. But it also reflected the unanticipated effects of other colonial regulations on the lives of women, and reactions to existing and changing gender relations in African societies that were driven by African men and women rather than white officials. To some extent, **indirect rule** meant 'colonial officials conspiring with older African men to exert control over women and junior men'. However, women were not completely powerless, and could not be entirely subordinated by colonial officials or African men. Female labour played an important part in colonial cash-crop economies, resulting in a tension between the wish to relegate women to the domestic sphere and the need to acknowledge their continuing economic role in the marketplace. Moreover, as established in Chapter 2, we should not exaggerate the ability of the colonial state to transform African society: it often had limited knowledge about, or ambition to change, the role of African women.[44]

The empire has also been presented as a key site for the forging of British and colonial masculinities and sexualities. Empire often created markedly 'homosocial' spaces, aboard ships, in army units, in educational institutions, on the margins of settled white society,

> connoting communities or societies not only composed solely of men, but exhibiting or endorsing behaviours or characteristics more readily associated – certainly historically – with men. Thus the rough and ready frontier societies of the settler colonies were not merely peopled in their early days almost exclusively by men, but were also characterized by hard drinking, lawlessness, and a disregard for polite social norms.[45]

In a different way, historians have also examined how empire created particular types of opportunities for homosexual relationships.

> Colonialism and imperialism, in theory, aimed to set up respectable, loyal and profitable European outposts overseas, and to impart European (generally Christian) virtues to 'savages' and 'heathen'; in this design, homosexuality had no place. Paradoxically, however, colonialism – to the horror of stay-at-home moralists – encouraged sexual irregularity, heterosexual and homosexual. Male bonding proved essential to the colonial adventure, especially on the frontier, during warfare and in the pioneer period preceding arrival of large numbers of European women. Confinement of lusty young men to military cantonments (or other same-sex milieux) created a hothouse of sexual urges, with trespassing across sexual borders bound to occur. Hierarchical relations – master to slave, entrepreneur to employee, officer to subaltern, colonist to houseboy – facilitated sexual expectations and demands. The relative wealth of Europeans overseas made the exchange of sex for money or other advantages easy.[46]

Recent work has meanwhile emphasized that empire worked to shape masculinity in mutually constitutive ways, linking Britain and its colonies. Mrinalini Sinha thus argues that ideas about masculinity in Britain and India flowed to and fro across the internal boundaries of the empire:

late nineteenth-century notions of English/British masculinity or Bengali/ Indian effeminacy cannot be understood simply from the framework of discrete 'national' cultures; instead they must be understood in relation to one another, and as constitutive of each other.[47]

Such understandings of masculinity were also influenced by ideas about race and class. British identity was, according to this argument, associated with 'those masculine attributes of energy, innovation and purposefulness associated with the gentry and upper middle classes, and required both of political leaders and of colonial administrators'.[48] Some groups of colonial subjects were meanwhile presented as effeminate and thus unsuited to military service, while others were seen as embodying masculine and gentlemanly virtues. These latter groups, 'martial races', were favoured by military recruiters for their proverbial strength and courage, and were drawn predominantly from areas that were perceived to be loyal to the colonial state. Here, race was used as 'a consciously manipulated linguistic and performative tool ... as an artificial strategy of rule during a period of imperial anxiety'. Ideas about the masculinity of martial races in India and elsewhere also corresponded with, and perhaps reinforced, ideas about military masculinity in Victorian Britain itself.[49]

Similarly, ideas about male and female gender roles in colonial settings were inevitably shaped in relation to one another. From the mid-nineteenth century onwards, some argued that overly masculine settler colonies needed to be tamed by exporting more white women to inhabit them. Women would 'domesticate' unruly colonial men, and replicate British gender structures in the colonies. From the 1850s, increasing number of white wives travelled to India to join their husbands: during the twentieth century, wives also joined male colonial officials in Africa. Gender and race relations may as a result have changed markedly compared with the early days of colonial rule, when sexual relations and concubinage between British men and non-European women predominated. In the Canadian West, for example,

> In the early years of the Canadian fur-trade, traders commonly married local women who brought to the marriage valuable trading networks as well as critical survival skills in a hostile climate. By the end of the eighteenth century, they favoured instead mixed-race women who moved more easily between the indigenous and the settler communities. By the middle of the nineteenth century, such partnerships were giving way to marriages between European men and women, as the idea of mixed-race sex became less and less palatable among both metropolitan and colonial whites.[50]

Historians of gender have thus argued that ideas and beliefs about the nature of men and women and their roles in the economy and in politics, society, and culture acted to shape the nature of empire. They have also argued that the imperial experience simultaneously transformed thinking about gender both in the colonies and in Britain itself. Influence flowed back and forth between metropole and colonies in a complex fashion. Joanna de Groot claims that there were direct 'structural connections' between Western male discourses about women and about non-Europeans: 'the theme of domination/subordination [was] central both to nineteenth-century masculine identity and to the Western sense of superiority'.[51] Ann Laura Stoler meanwhile argues that empire was a crucial site for the production of European sexuality.[52] Empire is thus held to have transformed thinking not just about the roles of women and men in non-European societies, but also about gender roles among whites living in the colonies and whites living back in Britain itself.[53] Such arguments tie in with wider attempts to write a **new imperial history**, and reflect the influence of Edward Said and other theorists of **postcolonialism**, who claim that empire played a crucial role in shaping the society and culture of the imperial powers.

▶ Conclusions

Historians have devoted a great deal of attention to exploring ideas about difference in imperial and colonial settings, and about hierarchies of race, class, caste, and gender. The result has been a rich new cultural history of empire, which reveals the imperial and colonial roots of many previously unexplored aspects of nineteenth- and twentieth-century British thought. Yet this research has also underscored (sometimes inadvertently) the complex and ambiguous nature of much of this contemporary thought, the contradictory ways in which people approached issues of difference at home and overseas. As a result, it is difficult to sustain arguments that depend on the concept of a hegemonic, widely accepted, and uncontested contemporary understanding of difference as a fundamental underpinning for empire at home and abroad.

It is also difficult to represent the British empire as a 'world-changing force', if by that term we mean something that fundamentally transformed non-European societies and cultures. If we define 'empire' in narrow terms, then it seems unlikely that colonial states generally had the power to undertake the root-and-branch destruction of African and Asian cultures and their replacement with new structures designed to facilitate colonial rule, or that colonial officials had the desire to do so in the first place. If we define 'empire' more broadly, or use the catch-all term 'colonialism', then we encounter further conceptual difficulties. Non-official agents of empire – missionaries, entrepreneurs, etc. – may have broadened and deepened the effects of British overseas expansion, but seldom seem to have exerted a wide-spread transformative influence over Asian and African societies. If we define empire or colonialism in still-broader terms, we are left facing a number of even more difficult questions. Where do we draw the line between imperial and non-imperial European influences on other societies and cultures? Is it helpful to label all European influence overseas, into the era of decolonization and perhaps beyond, as colonialism? If we do adopt this position, do we risk losing our ability to understand the fine-grained differences of motive, intention, and authority that drove various groups of people in their overseas activities? Will we end up denying non-Europeans any real ability to shape the imperial and colonial presence, to resist it, or to turn it to their own ends and serve their own agendas? If we reduce everything to a singular process of colonialism, then how can we judge the relative significance of the varied influences emanating from the British overseas presence, of the many forces generated within indigenous societies (and bridging the pre-colonial, colonial, and post-colonial eras), and of transnational connections that were not obviously the product of any sort of imperial presence?

Andrew Porter has usefully discussed some of the conceptual difficulties generated by debates about the cultural transformations brought by empire. For Porter, accounts which stress the profound and transformative effects of empire assume, often implicitly, the existence of pristine cultures outside Europe which, without empires or their agents, would have continued to exist in some ideal and untouched state. This is not a very realistic picture of cultural interaction and change. A wide range of expansive forces, emanating from both Europe and the non-European world, had been bringing different cultures into contact and interaction for centuries before the extension of colonial rule. Moreover, accounts which stress the transformative effects of empire tend to apply the label of 'cultural imperialism' to 'any instance where awareness of the wider world represented by the West has influenced indigenous cultural change'.[54] Rather than seek to measure the relative strength or to contextualize the transformative effects of different European influences on other places, such histories aggregate all types of European influences under the unhelpful umbrella term 'colonialism'. This problem, according to Porter, arises from

> a shared but problematical assumption. It is that cultures, whether approached at particular levels or taken in their entirety, are essentially and wholly coherent, organic structures. Each part is integral to the whole; its alteration, suppression, or removal presents a serious threat, a significant source of cultural damage. This represents the persistence of an older anthropological perspective on societies, in which perhaps at least traces can be sensed of that hankering after the supposedly pure, unadulterated, virtually unchanging 'culture' of an

age before Europeans and colonialists arrived. It is allied to an outlook inclined to regard change, unless evidently generated in an entirely endogenous, supposedly 'natural' fashion, as a sign of corruption and deprivation. Who would not, after all, prefer 'the real thing'?

Porter argues instead that we should see 'cultures' as

> relatively loosely-structured systems, in which the transference of customs or ideas and their adaptation to new and different purposes (perhaps not readily appreciated by European observers) is often a ready response to the experience of culture contact. The freedom for individuals or sub-groups to adapt in various ways to external opportunities and inspiration, and the capacity of the society to which they belong for assimilating or tolerating those changes, are significantly greater in this more 'robust' model of culture and its formation.[55]

Non-European cultures were flexible and varied, and had already been shaped by a range of conflicts, which European agents interacted with and sometimes influenced.

Similarly, according to this perspective we should refrain from exaggerating either the dominance or the monolithic nature of British culture. Diverse British influences acted on varied colonial societies and cultures, through processes that involved bargaining, negotiation, violence, and dispossession. Often, the colonial encounter left room for subjects to pursue their own agendas and to shape the nature of colonial rule, sometimes to their own advantage, although the balance of power could shift markedly over time and from place to place. As the wide applicability of the concept of **collaboration** reminds us, colonial rule always relied on the willingness of some subjects to work with the colonial state. Colonial rule had to offer those subjects some measure of power if they were to operate effectively, and this often determined the way that colonial rulers approached and worked with inherited precolonial categories of difference.

4 Identity

▶ Differentiation *versus* integration

Historians have demonstrated that the British empire perpetuated, created, and was sustained by difference. However, their research has also shown that there were clear limits to these processes of differentiation. As discussed in the previous chapter, colonial rule may have been facilitated by policies consciously aimed at dividing colonial subjects up into different and opposing groups, creating hierarchies among those groups, and stressing the unbridgeable chasm between colonial subjects and their British rulers. The exacerbation of divisions of class, caste, race, and gender played a part in this process. Yet in practice the colonial state was often unable to reach deeply enough into colonial societies to effect such transformations. Indigenous influences thus continued to play a key role in shaping social structures and identities across Asia, Africa, and the Pacific.

Indeed, we could go further than this, and argue that there was in fact no direct and necessary connection between the production of difference and the requirements of colonial rule. Although Jane Burbank and Frederick Cooper argue that empires, by their very nature, worked by treating different groups of subjects in different ways, they acknowledge that in practice 'All empires were to some degree reliant on both incorporation and differentiation.'[1] At times empires might act to divide people, but they also had to bring diverse groups together, creating cultural affinities and encouraging social integration and a measure of consent. Empires that failed to do this, and that relied entirely on repression, could not last for long. This integrative function is one of the least theorized and most neglected of the organizing concepts required for an understanding of imperial history.

In some ways, the production of difference might have worked against the requirements of colonial rule. The production of difference could be interpreted as an irrational phenomenon, undermining the long-term durability of empire, rather than as a rational tool of colonial authority. Exaggerating the differences between groups of colonial subjects always ran the risk of encouraging civil disorder. **Communalism**, fierce hatreds between different religious, ethnic, or linguistic groups expressed through violence and/or constitutional political mobilization, emerged as a major threat to continued, stable imperial rule, particularly during the first half of the twentieth century. Moreover, Partha Chatterjee's 'rule of colonial difference', the idea of an unbridgeable gap between white rulers and colonial subjects, did not just legitimate empire: it could also be cited by those who wished to justify the end of empire.[2] At a basic level, nationalists claimed that colonial subjects were fundamentally different from their white rulers, and that colonial authority was thus illegitimate. They turned the rule of colonial difference back against their overlords.

Communalism and nationalism are key concepts that have become central to much writing about empire and decolonization, and need to be considered carefully in any discussion of differentiation and integration.

In the second half of the twentieth century, many historians tended to assume the existence of a simple antagonism between imperialism and nationalism. They regarded nationalism as the solvent of empire. From 1914 onwards, the British empire seemed to have been fatally undermined by the rise of nationalism among its colonial subjects. In Ireland and Egypt nationalist resistance forced a partial imperial withdrawal in the wake of the First World War. In India and Palestine, **communalism** and nationalism together posed an intensifying threat to colonial rule during the interwar period, and encouraged a British retreat immediately after the Second World War. In the decades that followed, a rising tide of nationalism (sometimes fortified by Communist ideology) seemed to drive the British out of their remaining Asian and African strongholds. As the British Prime Minister Harold Macmillan put it in 1960, the 'winds of change' were sweeping through Africa: nationalism was an irresistible force that colonial rulers or white supremacists (he was speaking in South Africa) opposed at their peril.[3] In the wake of these dramatic changes, imperial loyalist identities seemed, at best, a form of false consciousness that had inevitably withered away when exposed to the genuine passion of national belonging. Colonial subjects had overcome the 'divide and rule' strategies of their imperial masters, and become conscious of their true national identities, in order to overthrow colonial rule. The belief that nationalism had triumphed over imperialism seemed to fit a post-1945 world in which nation-states had taken the place of colonies. Such assumptions also suited the successor states established after the end of colonial rule, which were often novel creations encompassing diverse populations. The story of a national struggle against imperial oppression was a helpful tool for contemporary nation-builders.

As we saw in Chapter 1, some of the key works that established much of the analytical framework for imperial history were written during the period of decolonization. The theories and concepts that they deployed were certainly influenced by an awareness of contemporary events, including the role seemingly being played by nationalist movements in driving Britain's withdrawal from empire. In their discussion of the Scramble for Africa, Ronald Robinson and John Gallagher sought to establish continuities with later decolonization, presenting nationalist resistance as a common theme linking the two periods. They thus argued that British territorial expansion was a response to 'nationalist crises' in South Africa and Egypt, which were in turn reactions to 'intensifying European influences during previous decades'. In the closing decades of the nineteenth century,

> All the processes of British expansion were reaching their peak. The metropolitan society was putting forth its strongest energies. It was at this climactic point that the social changes in its satellites were quickest and most violent. Hence it was at this time that their relations with the metropolis tended to move into crisis. The colonial communities were breaking off toward full independence; while anti-western nationalism and social upheaval were estranging the non-European partners of British interests.

Formal and **informal empire** were bringing the 'modernization' of the colonies, and inevitably stimulating nationalist resistance as they did so. British policy-makers thus turned to 'pre-nationalist' local elites as more manageable collaborators: 'Indian princes, Egyptian pashas or African paramount chiefs'.[4] Later, Robinson argued that **decolonization** eventually occurred when nationalists were able to persuade these local elites to cease their **collaboration** with the British, and instead to unify behind a new order: 'when the colonial rulers had run out of indigenous collaborators, they either chose to leave or were compelled to go'.[5] By implication, we might also explain **decolonization** in terms of the declining ability of Britain to offer the resources that would-be collaborators required, to make the bargain seem worthwhile to both parties. This might also help explain the drift of the settler empire out of the British embrace in the wake of the Second World War.

In some ways, this account chimes with modernist theories which present nationalism as the product of nineteenth- and twentieth-century social change: industrialization, urbanization, the growth of state power, and the rise of the mass media.[6] As British commercial interests and colonial states combined to encourage the economic transformation of the colonies, colonial nationalism emerged to hasten the end of colonial rule and the transfer of authority to indigenous rulers. This account echoes histories that, as we saw in Chapter 1, present empire as a temporary state-building expedient, that abolished itself when no longer required. Yet, as much of the analysis in this book has argued, the impact of British business and colonial rule on Asian and African societies and economies was often limited. Before the Second World

War, with the exception of the settler colonies and small trading outposts else-where, colonial states seldom had either the desire or the ability to enter into large-scale projects of 'modernization' and economic development. In India, colonial rule may have acted to 'traditionalize' social and economic structures.

A more useful aspect of **modernist theories of nationalism** is their insistence that national identities are not natural growths, the consequence of some mystical inner spirit of a people, but are social constructs. Conscious ideological work is required in order to make people believe that they are part of a nation, and that their nation requires a state of its own in order to realize its full potential. National communities are 'imagined', and are imagined for a purpose, perhaps to serve the needs of capital for bigger and more homog-enous markets, or of a state that wishes to mobilize its resources more effec-tively without causing social unrest. According to this viewpoint, national identities are no more authentic than imperial ones. Both have to be con-structed actively, involving ideological effort, and both are liable to erosion. Indeed, national and imperial identities may not have been polar opposites, locked in a struggle in which nationalism was bound to triumph: histories of identity in the British empire are more complex than this simple model would have us believe. As Christopher Bayly has argued, imperialism and nationalism were often tightly entangled, sometimes working in a mutually supportive way rather than in an oppositional, antagonistic fashion.[7]

This chapter looks at how national and imperial identities were constructed in the British empire. It starts by focusing on the case of Indian nationalism, and on debates about how and why all-India nationalist political organization developed during the late nineteenth and twentieth centuries. It then consid-ers identity formation in Asia and Africa more widely, before turning to the impact of empire on British identities. Here, it examines accounts that present empire as having played a crucial role in influencing British culture and iden-tity, and also looks at how some historians have critiqued such work. Finally, it considers the creation and erosion in the nineteenth and twentieth centuries of an imperial British identity, encompassing a 'British world' that stretched from Britain to the settler colonies and beyond.

▶ **Empire and identity in Asia and Africa**

Much historical work on identity in the British empire has emphasized the development of nationalist resistance, and its role in overturning colonial rule. As we saw in the previous chapter, in the wake of independence historians of India tended to present a Manichean struggle between the *raj* and Indian nationalism. According to this interpretation, the British empire frustrated

South Asian national aspirations, and nationalist leaders eventually rose up to overthrow its malign influence, resulting in the creation of an independent nation-state (or rather, two states – India and Pakistan). While most historians would acknowledge that there is some truth in this basic picture, a much more nuanced and complex depiction of the relationship between nationalism and imperialism in India has been offered by both the Cambridge school and Subaltern Studies.

As discussed in Chapter 2, the Cambridge school emphasized that the British *raj* was built on Indian **collaboration**. According to Anil Seal, several factors worked to unsettle colonial rule. The emergence of a growing body of Western-educated Indians, with limited opportunities for employment, led to an ever-increasing demand for greater access to positions in public service. For Seal, the roots of Indian nationalism lay not in opposition to the colonial state, but in demands for increased participation in the running of that state. Educated Indians were demanding more opportunities to collaborate and reap the rewards of **collaboration**: they were not seeking to terminate collaborative relationships. It was the unwillingness of the British to admit the legitimacy of such claims that pushed educated Indians into anti-colonial nationalism.[8]

Seal, along with other historians of the Cambridge school, also offered a provocative set of arguments to explain how a wider range of local and provincial groups and their grievances became linked up into a broader nationalist movement. All-India political activism, the Cambridge school argued, resulted neither from the intrinsic appeal of nationalist ideology nor from the integrating effects of economic and social 'modernization'. Rather, it was a response to patterns set by the colonial government. In the later nineteenth century, driven by the need to meet the rising costs of the army, administration, and infrastructural projects, the colonial state made new revenue demands of peasants. This in turn necessitated placing greater responsibilities and burdens on the shoulders of Indians collaborators, on local and provincial administrators. In return, collaborators demanded an increased role in the running of the state, through nominated and elected positions in government. As the state worked on an increasingly all-India level during this period, centralizing power and applying more uniform policies across the sub-continent, so Indians responded by developing national political structures of their own in order to make their demands for participation heard. 'Imperialism built a system which interlocked its rule in locality, province and nation; nationalism emerged as a matching structure of politics.'[9] Imperialism and nationalism were thus symbiotically linked. Indeed, Seal argued that the long, half-hearted, and often inconclusive struggle between the *raj* and Indian nationalists reflected the fact that imperialism and nationalism were ultimately different means of achieving much the same ends.

[Both] set about modernising the societies under its control; nationalism has sought to conserve the standing of some of those elites which imperialism had earlier raised up or confirmed; at various times both have worked to win the support of the same allies. In India they have sometimes achieved similar results as well: each in its own fashion sharpening the rivalries that were already stirring in the country; each grappled with the countervailing forces thrown up by the unevennesses of Indian society, and by the mobilisation of further ranges of its population.[10]

The Cambridge school's arguments that the *raj* was based on Indian **collaboration**, that much of early Indian political activity centred around competition for opportunities to collaborate, and that it was the colonial state that provided the main impetus for Indians to organize on an all-India basis, have been strongly contested by some other scholars. Partha Chatterjee, who as we have seen emphasizes that the *raj* was founded on racial difference rather than **collaboration**, argues that the focus of the Cambridge school on all-India political activity misses the most significant aspects of early Indian nationalism. For Chatterjee, the initial task of Indian nationalism was to 'overcome the subordination of the colonized middle class' and challenge ideas about the racial superiority of the white colonial rulers. For Chatterjee, anti-colonial nationalists in Asia and Africa first sought to subvert the colonial order in the realm of culture, of the 'spiritual', before going on to target the explicitly political aspects of colonial rule, the domain of 'the economy and of statecraft, of science and technology'.[11]

Nevertheless, many scholars have followed the lead offered by the Cambridge school, rejecting the idea of a simple opposition between nationalism and imperialism, and instead drawing out the complexity of the history of identity formation in colonial Asia and Africa. Their work raises questions that bring us back into the difficult conceptual territory encountered at the end of the previous chapter. How far should we see cultural change in Britain's colonies as the direct outcome of 'colonialism'? Did the changes that occurred in Asian and African societies reflect the conscious policies or unconscious motives of colonial administrators or of the various non-official agents of British influence? Or were locally generated, indigenous forces driving change? Indeed, were colonial subjects and rulers alike swept up in larger, global processes of change that transcended anything that could be identified as 'colonialism'?

One thing is clear: we cannot use 'colonialism' and 'Westernization' as synonyms. Non-European societies had begun to adopt and adapt elements of Western culture well before the spread of informal imperial influence or formal rule, and continued to do so after **decolonization** and the end of empire. Countries which never became colonies, such as Japan, were still deeply affected by Western cultural influences.[12] As John Darwin puts it,

Empire – as foreign rule – was an agent of cultural change. But it was only one among several. It often arrived in harness with others: the expansion of trade; new kinds of consumption; swifter methods of transport; the codification of language in script; the widening of literacy; new communications techniques, including regular letter post and the telegraph; new kinds of schooling; new forms of literature, not least newspapers and pamphlets; new medical knowledge; new notions of leisure and taste; a different and demanding religion. Some or all might arrive in a region before empire itself and sprung from local initiative: the best example is Egypt. Empire might act to strengthen the impact of such changes and exploit their potential for imperial advantage. But its men on the spot just as often displayed a timid desire to shore up the old order, both cultural and political.[13]

Historians have recognized these problems, and have generally ceased to describe cultural change in Britain's colonies in terms of 'cultural imperialism'. The virtual disappearance of this concept from historical writing is an acknowledgement of the complex and obscure nature of the connections between empire and cultural change. As we have seen, historians now often prefer to think about hybridity, and to acknowledge the role of colonial subjects in transforming cultural influences from Europe and the US, turning them to their own purposes.[14] The concept of cultural imperialism implies a too-direct connection between imperial power and cultural change.

Cultural change in Asia under colonial rule was certainly significant, but did not erase or entirely transform pre-colonial cultures and identities, and did not necessarily follow the lines anticipated by British administrators and social reformers. Neither can cultural change be attributed entirely, or perhaps even principally, to broader European influences. Change took place as the result of complex webs of long-term interaction linking Asian colonies with Europe, but also with other Asian societies. Internally generated dynamics of change were highly significant too. Social and cultural change was most marked in large port-cities like Calcutta, Bombay, Singapore, Hong Kong, and Rangoon. In these colonial centres English-speaking Asian bureaucrats, professionals, and entrepreneurs formed dynamic communities that often embraced new technologies and media to strengthen political and cultural campaigns for reform. In Malaya, for example, Straits-born Chinese elites used the English-language press to campaign for political inclusion and to advance their own social and cultural agendas. English-language newspapers seemed to offer opportunities to connect with comparable movements around the globe, and potentially to unify the diverse groups which inhabited the colony. 'Between the sunset of empire and the dawn of nationalism lay the hopeful twilight of cosmopolitanism.'[15] In these Asian port-cities, large, urban, working-class populations also developed,

and sustained rich popular cultures. The overall result was 'a kind of negotiated arms-length encounter which both absorbed and contained the effects of
"modernity"'. It was not clear that the outcomes of this encounter served the
needs of the colonial state or British business. Indeed, the opposite may have
been the case:

> 'Modernity' in education and culture was ... not widely thought to have
> brought stability and social harmony to the Empire. By 1914 many Britons had
> realized that the more their Asian subjects travelled, prospered, and educated
> themselves, the less they were inclined to see themselves as living in a self-
> contained or uncontested world of British power and influence.[16]

British observers thus tended to reject these new urban cultures as undesirable
and inauthentic.

Some historians have identified similar patterns operating in Britain's colonies in tropical Africa. Creole elites in Britain's coastal enclaves developed
complex hybrid identities: adopting and adapting ideas about Britishness; converting to Christianity; stressing their loyalty to the British monarchy; taking up
British sports and other pastimes; seeking a British-style education, locally or in
Britain itself; and claiming the political rights of 'black Englishmen'. Elements
of this hybrid culture also emerged in the West Indies, where the adoption
of cricket and its associated values was among the most prominent outward
signs of the British connection, and where 'the main focus of working-class
loyalty remained the British monarchy which was first associated with slave
emancipation'.[17] Black West Indians, like other colonial subjects, 'conceptual-
ized, identified with, and manipulated their own versions of Britishness, and in
so doing played a profound (and hitherto neglected) role in British history'.[18]

To some extent, policy-makers accepted in theory the claims of black subjects
to membership of an imperial British community of equals, particularly when
they desired administrative or military service from those black subjects. [19]
In practice, however, the claims of black subjects about their Britishness were
never entirely endorsed. In particular, from the mid-nineteenth century imperial and colonial administrators became more likely to reject creole claims to
political equality. Increasingly, they treated these groups as inauthentic 'mimic
men', as less desirable or authentic collaborators compared to 'traditional'
African leaders.[20] In South Africa, white settlers meanwhile created an increasingly segregationist system of race relations, progressively eroding the status
of Cape Coloureds, and denying political and economic freedoms to blacks.
Many Cape Coloureds and blacks supported the British effort in the South
African War of 1899–1902. This reflected genuine British loyalties, and also a
more instrumental sense that imperial intervention offered their best hope of

regaining lost rights and land, and of preventing the fiercely unequal values and structures of the Boer republics spreading into the British colonies. Black and Coloured hopes were to be dashed after the war, as the British government handed power to the settler-dominated, increasingly segregationist government of the new Union of South Africa. Yet empire loyalism continued to be a prominent feature of black and Coloured political activism, even as the foundations of *apartheid* were being put into place.[21]

Finally, it is worth noting that the theories concerning the emergence of colonial nationalism devised by the Cambridge school to explain the relationship between Indian political organization and colonial rule have also been applied to Africa. John Gallagher thus claimed that nationalism in tropical Africa after the Second World War had been called into being by the British post-war colonial development drive and the increasing interventionism of the colonial state. As in India, when the colonial state tried to govern on a country-wide basis, it united local grievances and encouraged local politicians to organize on a national scale.[22]

As John Darwin has concluded, Western ideas had an enormous impact on Asian and African societies in this period, but these ideas were not simply imposed by agents of the West in order to facilitate colonial rule and exploitation. Asians and Africans actively and often enthusiastically adopted those elements of Western culture that seemed useful or appealing, and turned them to their own ends. Sometimes this did not work in the interests of Britain or its colonial states: 'exactly the weapons through which Western ideas were so widely diffused – the print media, cheap travel and educational institutions – could be turned to the tasks of cultural renovation and resistance'.[23] Again, the relationship between nationalism and imperialism was complex and in constant flux.

▶ **Empire and identity in Britain**

Historians have also been concerned to explore the impact of empire on British culture and identity. Some have portrayed empire as a significant tool of social integration in Britain: the basis of a sense of national identity or racial superiority that drew all the social classes together; a joint enterprise that helped bind the 'four nations' of England, Scotland, Ireland, and Wales into the United Kingdom; or perhaps a means to cement the **hegemony** of the elite and convince the working classes of the merits of a social order in which they occupied a subordinate and disadvantaged position. Drawing on **modernist theories of nationalism**, from this perspective we might understand support and enthusiasm for empire as Britain's version of 'official nationalism', an ideology endorsed by the government that bolstered the authority of the state and the ruling elite.[24]

The argument that expansion overseas could be used to defuse social tensions at home has a long pedigree. As we saw in Chapter 1, one of J. A. Hobson's main objections to overseas expansion as set out in his book *Imperialism: a Study* was the potential it offered to distract the working classes from their own plight and from the possibilities of social reform. This harked back to Marx's use of the word 'imperialism' to describe the showy adventurism of Napoleon III in France. In the early twentieth century, some called this 'social imperialism'.[25]

However, while historians have looked hard for evidence of social imperialist manipulation of the masses by British politicians, little has been forthcoming. Freda Harcourt attempted to prove that Benjamin Disraeli was Britain's social imperialist *par excellence*. Disraeli masterminded the Abyssinian expedition of 1867, a major British military operation deploying overwhelming and disproportionate force, dispatched ostensibly to free a handful of British subjects held captive by the Abyssinian Emperor. According to Harcourt, the expedition was in fact primarily a piece of political showmanship, an opportunity to stoke the fires of patriotism and demonstrate the supremacy of Britain and the competence of its governing elite. Saturation press coverage was crucial in ensuring that the expedition succeeded in its real objective. Unfortunately, Harcourt did not find a 'smoking gun' in the archives to support this argument, a piece of paper that proved Disraeli's intentions. Her evidence for Disraelian social imperialism was instead circumstantial, consisting of newspaper and periodical articles and other contemporary literature, broadly suggestive of an atmosphere, rather than proof of an actual policy.[26]

John MacKenzie and Stephen Howe have both since acknowledged that there is little evidence to suggest that Disraeli or any other British politician of the late nineteenth or early twentieth century was a 'social-imperialist puppetmaster' akin to Bismarck in Germany.[27] Some contemporary politicians and imperial enthusiasts may have claimed that empire could ameliorate poverty and social tensions at home, but it would be hard to prove that such arguments swayed policy-makers when considering any specific instance of territorial expansion. As with plans to promote the economic development of the colonies, the possibilities of social imperialism may have become apparent more as a consequence than a cause of expansion. In the early twentieth century the British Colonial Secretary Joseph Chamberlain and other 'constructive imperialists' sought to make the British public more 'empire minded'. Chamberlain's Tariff Reform campaign, launched in 1903 and seeking to bind the empire together into a more autarkic economic unit, certainly drew on ideas about using trade with the empire to improve the condition of the British working classes. But this was a project of imperial consolidation, rather than expansion. In his earlier, aggressive treatment of the Boer republics of Southern Africa that culminated in the war of 1899–1902, there is little to suggest that Chamberlain was driven by a social imperialist agenda.[28]

In accounting for the outbreak of the South African War, Hobson believed that a pre-existing, largely irrational popular enthusiasm for imperial expansion had pushed British policy-makers towards conflict. Hobson thought that this 'jingoism' had helped bring about the war. This word had entered into popular usage in 1877, during a diplomatic clash with Russia. An immensely popular music hall song, 'By Jingo!', had included the famous lines:

> We don't want to fight, but by Jingo if we do,
> We've got the men, we've got the ships, we've got the money too.
> We've fought the Bear before, and while we're Britons true,
> The Russians shall not have Constantinople.[29]

The word 'jingo' came to be applied to enthusiastic backers of a forceful foreign policy, advocates of war and empire. Hobson defined jingoism as 'That inverted patriotism whereby the love of one's own nation is transformed into the hatred of another nation, and the fierce craving to destroy the individual members of that other nation.'[30]

Hobson thought that jingoism was a consequence of the conditions of modern, urban life. New transport and communications technologies meant that people had come under 'the direct influence of a thousand times as many other persons as were their ancestors before the age of steam and electricity'. Urbanization and industrial employment had meanwhile combined to 'destroy or impair independence of character, without substituting any sound, rational sociality'. The working classes had become even more suggestible than in the past:

> The neurotic temperament generated by town life seeks natural relief in stormy sensational appeals, and the crowded life of the streets, or other public gatherings, gives the best medium for communicating them. This is the very atmosphere of Jingoism. A coarse patriotism, fed by the wildest rumours and the most violent appeals to hate and the animal lust of blood, passes by quick contagion through the crowded life of cities, and recommends itself everywhere by the satisfaction it affords to sensational cravings.[31]

The new, mass-circulation press pandered to the blood-lust of the mob, and provided the means by which interest groups could harness popular prejudice to schemes of imperial expansion.

The appearance of hard truth imparted by the mechanical rigidity of print possesses a degree of credit which, when the statement is repeated with sufficient frequency, becomes well-nigh absolute. No evidence is essential: the bare dogmatic statement, though emanating from an admittedly interested source, produces conviction and moves to action. How great a power is here placed in the control of a commercial clique or a political party, or any body of rich, able, and energetic men desirous to impose a general belief and a general policy upon the mass of the people![32]

Here, Hobson's theories about jingoism intersected with his wider arguments about the nature of imperialism, discussed above in Chapter 1. Hobson believed that imperialism ultimately served the interest of parasitic economic interest groups, and reflected the degree to which they had succeeded in bending the state to their will. He argued that the press had been one of the key means by which South African mining magnates had fed the British public with propaganda, harnessing jingoism and stoking up popular support for the war against the Boer republics. By 'combination and reiteration' the press 'had fastened a misjudgement, an exaggeration, or too frequently a falsehood, upon the public mind'.[33]

As discussed in Chapter 1, few historians would now concur wholeheartedly with Hobson's conspiracy theories. Recent work has similarly downplayed the significance of manipulation of the press by the mining industry during the South African War.[34] Nevertheless, many historians do agree that the economic benefits of empire were confined to a few key groups in British society, and that those commercial interests that did profit from empire played an active role in building up popular imperialism, encouraging the working classes to support overseas expansion even though it brought the masses few material rewards.

John MacKenzie has been foremost among those arguing that public support for empire in Britain, and indeed across Europe, was broadly based. For MacKenzie, the popularization of empire was made possible, if not necessarily caused in any simple way, by the spread of education, literacy, the franchise, mass politics, organized entertainment, advertising aimed at mass markets, and popular newspapers and other forms of mass print culture.[35] According to MacKenzie, while the British state did little to attempt to popularize empire before the First World War, a range of private and semi-state 'imperial propagandist agencies' stepped into the breach. Companies used stereotyped images of the colonies and of their inhabitants to sell exotic imported products. Their national campaigns to market branded goods may have disseminated some of the most enduring images of empire. Schools, publishers of juvenile literature, youth movements such as the Boy Scouts, patriotic societies, the military, churches and missionary societies, music halls, exhibitions, and later radio and cinema all also shaped British understandings of Africa and Asia and their peoples, and strengthened 'an imperial nationalism, compounded of monarchism, militarism, and Social Darwinism, through which the British defined their own unique superiority *vis-à-vis* the rest of the world'. Imperial propaganda generated profits and influence for the companies and organizations that produced it, and also had a broader, socially conservative, impact. For MacKenzie, such propaganda created a form of false consciousness, encouraging the general public to support the defence of an empire which in fact only benefited the privileged few.[36] According to MacKenzie, working-class audiences took the bait offered by their masters, and bought into the imperial mind-set, even if they lacked a detailed knowledge of empire. Drawing on the Gramscian theories discussed above in Chapter 2, Stephen Heathorn has similarly presented empire as part of an 'hegemonic nationalist ideology', deeply rooted in prevalent working-class attitudes.[37]

An alternative approach to this same issue has meanwhile come from a number of practitioners of the **new imperial history**. As we have already seen, one of the ideas that brings this group of scholars together is the claim that Britain itself was profoundly shaped by empire. Many now profess a desire to see Britain and its colonies in 'one analytic field', interacting in a reciprocal and mutually constitutive (if also fundamentally unequal) way.[38] One consequence of this approach is the argument that British (or sometimes, more narrowly, English) national identity was the product of empire.

Here, early inspiration was provided by Linda Colley's work on the forging of British identity in the late eighteenth and early nineteenth centuries. Colley's work was influenced by an awareness of the fragile and contingent nature of British identity in an age of political devolution: she was writing about the making of the United Kingdom at the same time as it seemed to be breaking up. Colley's work also drew on **modernist theories of nationalism**, on an understanding of British identity as something that was actively constructed and imagined. Most significantly, for our purposes, Colley urged British historians to reject an introspective view of the national past, and instead to regard Britain as 'a one-time great power influencing and being influenced by every continent on the world'. Colley argued that British national identity was a product of the eighteenth- and early nineteenth-century wars against the French. Catholics overseas (and to some extent in Ireland) and subjects of 'the global empire won by way of these wars' had become the 'Other' against which English, Scottish, and Welsh defined their British identity.

> Whatever their own differences, Britons could feel united in dominion over, and in distinction from, the millions of colonial subjects beyond their own boundaries. It was no coincidence at all that the period of British imperial takeoff and success also witnessed the forging of an authentically British governing elite.

Colley's work suggested that Britishness at home was being 'forged' at exactly the same time that Britain was expanding overseas, that Britishness and the British empire were the product of the same historical moment.[39]

Building on these insights, Katherine Wilson has argued that the expansion of knowledge about the world and its inhabitants during the eighteenth and early nineteenth centuries informed and unsettled a developing sense of British identity. Britons encountered a wide range of peoples: they minimized their differences from some, and exaggerating their differences from others, to help forge their own identity.[40]

Historians such as Antoinette Burton and Catherine Hall have since argued that, through the operation of processes of **othering** in an imperial context, the British defined themselves in opposition to their colonial subjects. British national identity thus came to be based on ideas about racial superiority, leaving an enduring legacy in contemporary Britain in terms of attitudes towards race and inequality. Burton claims that empire was 'not just a phenomenon "out there," but a fundamental and constitutive part of English culture and national identity at home'.[41] Such arguments reflect the influence of Edward Said's belief that 'Orientalism' involved not only the creation of negative, racialized stereotypes about non-Europeans that could be used to justify their oppression and dispossession, but also the emergence of a corresponding set of beliefs by which Europeans sought to explain their own superiority in racial, stereotypical terms.[42]

Catherine Hall has similarly focused attention upon the role of empire in shaping British political discourses of nationhood, arguing that 'Nation ... as constituted in Britain in the nineteenth century, cannot be understood outside of empire.' According to Hall, during the debates leading up to the 1832 Reform Act, definitions of who was and who was not to be included in the nation were influenced by 'the construction of imagined others' in Ireland and Jamaica.[43] Similarly, Hall has claimed that subsequent events in Ireland and Jamaica (Fenian violence in 1867 and the Morant Bay rising of 1865 respectively) had a significant effect upon British political discourse and identity, especially regarding issues of race and gender.[44]

Hall has pursued these themes at greater length in her book *Civilising Subjects*, which argues 'that colony and metropole are terms which can be understood only in relation to each other, and that the identity of coloniser is a constitutive part of Englishness'. Hall focuses on connections between Jamaica and England, and more specifically upon links between Baptist missionaries in Birmingham and Jamaica. According to Hall, such bonds were 'mutually constitutive', shaping both 'coloniser and colonised', albeit in a process in which the 'coloniser' was generally holding the reins. As racial attitudes hardened from the mid-nineteenth century onwards, a new generation of thinkers (epitomized by Charles Dilke and his 1868 study of *Greater Britain*) came not only to view the capabilities of black people in racial terms, but also to view Europeans – or Anglo-Saxons, or Britons, or even the English – as a distinctive, and distinctly superior, race.[45] Hall has since claimed that empire was 'omnipresent in the everyday lives of "ordinary people"', joining with 'racial thought' to form a background of 'banal nationalism' that was too familiar to be worth remarking on by contemporaries most of the time, but no less potent for that.[46]

However, some other historians have directly refuted claims that empire transformed British culture and national identity. Bernard Porter has argued that the extent of imperial propaganda has been grossly exaggerated for the period prior to the 1880s, and that during subsequent decades the British working class resisted and rejected the rising tide of imperial persuasion. Porter argues that identification with empire was generally restricted to a relatively isolated upper-class elite within British society. Even within this group, enthusiasm for an overseas role was more a reflection of domestic traditions of rule than of dedication to empire *per se*. The middle classes were generally unenthusiastic about empire and resistant to imperial propaganda that sought to persuade them to change their minds. Working-class culture was even more resilient.

> Those who say ... that imperialism pervaded British culture and society generally during this period, are simply wrong. Either that, or they are deliberately excluding the 70–80 per cent of people who made up the Victorian *working* classes.... There is no direct evidence that this great majority of Britons supported the empire, took an interest in it, or were even aware of it for most of the century; whereas much circumstantial evidence points the other way.[47]

Porter argues that even if empire brought material changes that influenced the way British people worked, ate, or dressed, this did not necessarily shape the way they thought and behaved. Empire did not bring a fundamental transformation to British society or identity.

In the realm of the history of ideas, Peter Mandler has meanwhile examined a wide body of contemporary writings about British identity. He argues that while British attitudes towards race may have shifted around the middle of the nineteenth century, this did not necessarily bring about a substantial or lasting change in how British thinkers saw themselves and the world around them. Mandler argues that we can detect a broad continuity in British thinking about identity, which saw Britain's pre-eminent position in the world as deriving primarily from superior British institutions (liberty, self-government, enterprise, free thought, and Protestant piety) rather than from any biological racial characteristics.[48]

Rather than argue that empire shaped British culture and identity in a single, clear, hegemonic fashion, it seems more likely that a wide range of impe- rial influences were at work on multiple British cultures and identities in the nineteenth and twentieth centuries.[49] As Peter Marshall has argued, while empire did influence British identity, reinforcing a 'hierarchical view of the world', we can only understand Britain's imperial experience if we acknowl- edge that different sections of British opinion responded to empire in very dif- ferent ways. Ambivalent and diverse reactions meant that, rather than bring about a wholesale transformation, empire tended to reinforce existing conflicts and tensions within British society, working in a 'reflexive' way, with rather than against the grain of British domestic development.[50]

Even within particular social classes, empire could mean different things to different groups. Among elites, diverse political philosophies helped gener- ate divergent colonial policies and modes of governance. Among the working classes, responses differed according to whether and how empire was encoun- tered at home, in the workplace, and during leisure time. Gender similarly acted to complicate the impact of empire, interacting in varied ways with divi- sions of race and class. In *The Empire Strikes Back?* Andrew Thompson looks at areas of British life which clearly did register the impact of empire, including the growth of certain professional bodies and trade unions, the fortunes of some industries, and the development of lower middle class life experiences and identities. However, he also notes groups whose responses to empire were ambiguous or apathetic, and identifies influences (particularly economic ones) which, while superficially 'imperial', were in some ways indistinguishable from Britain's broader engagement with the outside world.[51]

In much the same way, the diversity of responses to empire becomes appar- ent if we move away from a too-conveniently narrow focus on 'Englishness', and think about wider British and Irish responses to empire. Empire might have been one of the things that helped bind the United Kingdom together, uniting the 'four nations' of England, Ireland, Scotland, and Wales in a com- mon endeavour. But perhaps more importantly, it provided a vast and capa- cious arena in which the different British and Irish national groups could pursue their own agendas and express their own identities. Enthusiasm for and participation in the expansion and administration of empire could form a key constituent of both Scottish Unionism and Scottish Nationalism, further complicating our thinking about the relationship between imperialism and nationalism.[52] The interaction between empire and identity in England, Ireland, Scotland, and Wales was subtle and complex. Research on the press suggests that different groups living in these islands engaged with imperial issues in very different ways, reflecting divergent domestic political viewpoints and very specific local perspectives.[53]

John Darwin thus emphasizes that '"empire" was understood in a variety of ways by people in Britain, and not just (or even very much) as the vicarious enjoyment of racial overlordship'. The empire was a destination for emigration: the 'settler' colonies promised the white working classes opportunities for economic advancement and greater political liberty. Empire was also associated with free trade in the nineteenth century, bringing mass consumer goods to Britain as well as luxuries for the elite. Empire meant military service overseas in the 'small wars' of the Victorian empire, but it was simultaneously linked to and shaped by Christian evangelicalism and humanitarian campaigning against slavery and acts of violence committed by troops and settlers against indigenous peoples.

> These different imaginings of empire – humanitarian, authoritarian, democratic, protectionist, free-trading, religious-minded and militaristic – existed because so many different interest groups in Britain saw it as an arena where their values and aims could be given expression. Empire, in that sense, was not so much a source of identity as a cockpit or battleground where different versions of Britishness competed for space.

Empire thus could hardly have generated a uniform, hegemonic version of British national identity. Rather, empire remained acceptable to a wide range of constituencies as a component part of British identities. Empire's loose hold on the British public also perhaps facilitated disengagement from the imperial past in the era of **decolonization**.[54]

▶ The British world

Thinking about British identity and empire has also recently led historians to develop the concept of the 'British world'. This historiographical movement partly emerged out of a sense that the existing theories used by imperial historians had neglected Britain's settler empire. They had little power to explain the nature of the imperial connection between Britain and its settler colonies, or of the imperial identities that linked Britons 'at home' and overseas for much of the nineteenth and twentieth centuries.[55] Historians are now doing much to reveal the connections that drew Britain, Canada, Australia, New Zealand, South Africa, and a range of other communities into a significant global grouping that was a sub-section both of the British empire and, from another perspective, of the English-speaking world.

Britishness 'at home' had the power to integrate English, Scottish, Welsh, and (to some extent) Irish people into an overarching political community, providing an identity that supplemented rather than replaced those of each of the 'four nations'. In the wider British world, Britishness could play a similar function, a means to supplement and even strengthen settler colonial identities and help bind people into imagined communities on several levels. Governments around the British world thus tended to buy into, rather than oppose, the British connection. Britishness was a form of 'official nationalism' in the settler colonies in much the same way as it was in Britain itself. Britishness was not something that was imposed on settlers from the imperial centre, but was as much their creation as it was that of Britons 'at home' in the United Kingdom.

An older literature on 'Anglo-Dominion relations' (by the end of the nineteenth century the self-governing settler colonies had become known as the 'white dominions' or simply the 'dominions') missed much of this, and instead presented the history of connections between Britain and the settler colonies in terms of a fundamental tension between imperialism and nationalism. This scholarship charted, and often celebrated, the gradual development of the settlers' relationship with Britain from one of near-total constitutional subservience to one of near-total autonomy. Initially, the end-point for the settler colonies of this evolutionary process had seemed to be equal status with Britain within a Commonwealth of self-governing partner nations. After the Second World War, the destination had become complete independence. As historians in Canada, Australia, and New Zealand focused on writing 'national histories' (South Africa, with its stark racial divisions and inequalities, always seemed a somewhat different case), they added little to this established narrative of constitutional history. Few attempts were made to apply new insights from the fields of social or cultural history to the study of the British connection.[56]

Yet, as historical scholarship is now emphasizing, contemporaries had not necessarily thought that they were moving along a path towards the disintegration of the connection between Britain and the dominions, or that there was a fundamental opposition between British imperialism and dominion nationalism. Writing in the early twentieth century, the imperial thinker Richard Jebb had argued that the growth of national identities in the settler colonies did not necessitate the termination of the imperial connection. Canada and Australia had come together as unitary states under the aegis of the empire: Jebb believed that 'the sheer fact of two great national unions having been accomplished shows that the British Empire, although it may delay, does not preclude the realization of national instincts'. Jebb urged British policy-makers to acknowledge the growth of such sentiment and to work in consultation and cooperation with settler leaders, rather than to try imposing British perspectives on them. Continued membership of the empire would then offer the settler states 'solid national advantages'.[57]

Jebb's writings drew on a broader strand in nineteenth-century Liberal thought, the idea that forms of nationalism that brought people together into ever-larger communities were a positive, constructive force. According to this viewpoint, the world had progressed from tribal to national structures, and would continue to move forward through the creation of larger regional and imperial units, and perhaps one day a single world government. British policy-makers had thus tended to look favourably upon the idea of bringing regional groupings of colonies together into larger 'national' federations. Such federations promised to assume more of the financial burden of colonial administration and military defence, and to offer the prospect of stable government and continued opportunities for British trade and investment.[58] By contrast, Jebb and many of his contemporaries viewed separatist forms of nationalism (of the type championed by Irish advanced nationalists, for example) as a retrograde, backward step towards 'tribalism'.[59]

During the 1960s and 1970s, an appreciation of the complexity of past attitudes towards questions of national and imperial unity led some historians to revise the earlier literature on Anglo-Dominion relations. In Canada, some historians re-examined the ideas of those who had advocated closer imperial unity, 'imperialists' as they called themselves. These historians argued that this label had in fact been a misnomer: in a Canadian setting, those who advocated continued, autonomous membership of the British empire as a means to counterbalance growing US influence in North America were actually better seen as early nationalists, rather than imperialists.[60] However, this was to some extent but another present-minded exercise in recovering the roots of contemporary Canadian nationalism. A more thought-provoking intervention came from Douglas Cole, who distinguished between nationalism, which he defined as a sentiment arising from perceived membership of a distinct people or ethnic group, and patriotism, defined as a loyalty to a territorial state and its institutions. Cole argued that what historians had commonly described as nationalism in Australia and Canada was in fact patriotism: an ideology focusing on winning autonomy for the state, and securing the loyalty of inhabitants to that state, rather than asserting the existence of any distinct ethnicity. Indeed, Cole argued that 'imperialists' in Canada, Australia, and New Zealand were in fact 'Britannic nationalists', subscribing to an identity based on ideas about a shared Anglo-Saxon heritage and continuing racial mission. It was possible to be a Britannic nationalist, accepting the idea of racial community with other parts of the empire, while also being a Canadian, Australian, or New Zealand patriot, championing the interests and autonomy of a local state.[61]

More recently, Neville Meaney and Stuart Ward have further refined these ideas. They argue that Britain and Australia were not always united in a 'community of interest': local needs diverged, and were championed by Australian patriots, even to the disadvantage of other parts of the empire. Nevertheless, Britain and Australia shared a 'community of culture' based around a Britannic nationalism that was not fundamentally challenged by quarrels over local interests.[62] Along with James Curran, Ward has also emphasized that much of the impetus for breaking the British connection came not from dominion nationalists, but rather from a Britain that increasingly saw its future as bound up with Europe, not the empire. Drawing on modernist theories about **invented tradition**, and looking at attempts in Australia to construct a 'new nationalism' to replace old Britannic identities, Curran and Ward argue that

> the ferment about refashioning the national image from the early 1960s to the 1980s represented not so much the stirring of a more 'authentically' Australian nationalism as a response to the relatively sudden collapse of Britishness as a credible totem of civic and sentimental allegiance in Australia.[63]

In many ways, Canada, Australia, and New Zealand found themselves moving in the post-war years not towards independence, but into a new relationship of cultural and military dependence upon the US.[64]

Historians are now building on these insights and writing new histories of imperial and national identities in the British world. This has involved paying closer attention to the wider connections that linked Britain and the settler colonies, in terms of trade, investment, military cooperation, political culture, and especially migration. Between 1815 and 1914, an estimated 22.6m people left Britain and Ireland. The majority went to the United States, but most of the rest went to Canada, Australia, New Zealand, and South Africa, in roughly that order of preference.[65] Migrants could be drawn suddenly in unprecedented numbers to particular areas, attracted by gold rushes or other booms, transforming urban and rural landscapes and human communities in remarkably short periods through what James Belich has called 'explosive colonisation'.[66] Some destinations attracted migrants from particular points of origin: Irish and Scottish migrants in particular tended to cluster, and proved particularly successful in preserving elements of the identities that they brought with them from the 'old country'. Migration also varied in intensity over time. The 15 years that preceded the First World War witnessed a noticeable spike in migration from Britain to Canada, as the prairie provinces were opened up to white settlement. This meant that on the eve of the war a greater percentage of the Canadian population was British-born than had been the case at the turn of the century, reinforcing the British connection.[67]

Migration created continuing cultural affinities between Britain and the dominions, strengthening political and economic bonds. As Gary Magee and Andrew Thompson have argued, emigration conditioned consumption habits within the colonies such that their tastes, expectations and values were readily familiar, communicable and comprehensible to manufacturers back in Britain; and it was emigration that enabled a rapid establishment of trust between commercial partners in the colonies and Britain, thereby facilitating long-distance trade.[68]

No less significant, and often the target for settler fears about the continued whiteness and Britishness of their communities, were the large numbers of black and Asian people who migrated into and around the British world.[69]

Historians working on the British world have stressed the complex, adaptive nature of connections between Britain and its settler offshoots. Migrants carried cultural, social, economic, and political practices with them to the dominions and to other enclaves of white sojourning and settlement around the empire. From an early stage policy-makers had sought to strengthen the Britishness of institutions in the settler colonies, and to reinforce the economic ties that linked them with Britain.[70] Some contemporaries also argued for state intervention to strengthen the demographic bridges that connected Britain and the dominions, to keep migrants within the empire and to prevent them from continuing to leach away to the independent United States. Nevertheless, despite these strong connections, British identities, ideas, and institutions were seldom replicated in unmodified form in the settler colonies.

This was certainly the case in the realm of political culture. In registering claims to be considered British, settlers were insisting that they had carried the rights of 'freeborn Englishmen' overseas with them: 'being British anywhere meant exercising full civil rights within a liberal, pluralistic polity, or at least aspiring to that status'.[71] But the meaning of those British political rights shifted in the settler colonies. In the dominions, British laws and institutions were imported selectively, reflecting the desire to build 'better Britains'.[72] Universal manhood suffrage was enacted much earlier in the dominions than it was in Britain, and pioneering labour legislation established Australia and New Zealand as a 'working man's paradise', at least relative to Britain. The extent of the political rights enjoyed by white colonial subjects in the self-governing dominions was particularly notable when contrasted with the case of Ireland. Women also enjoyed enhanced political and economic status in the dominions, and achieved political equality with men sooner than did their counterparts in Britain. By the early twentieth century, some British Liberals had even come to see the dominions as a useful repository of British liberty, which could be drawn on (through legislative borrowing) to reinvigorate political culture at home. Influences from the dominions could thus be exported to Britain: the British world was built on multiple and often reciprocal connections.

Imperial institutions which sought to work within this British world could not simply project a metropolitan version of Britishness upon it. They had to enter into complex and sometimes fraught negotiations with institutions and audiences in Canada, Australia, New Zealand, and South Africa, and adapt their operations to suit local requirements. The history of the British Broadcasting Corporation's empire broadcasting efforts offers an excellent illustration of this: the BBC had to nurture carefully a whole set of relationships with broadcasters overseas, and hone its programmes to harmonize closely with local tastes and requirements.[73] In other fields, similarly complex and reciprocal structures of interconnection were created: for example, universities in Britain and the settler colonies became linked in a myriad of ways, establishing a 'British academic world'.[74]

To some extent, Britannic nationalism was based on a sense of racial identity, drawing on contemporary beliefs about the Anglo-Saxon origins and virtues of the British. From an early stage, white settlers had deployed ideas about race and British identity that 'played a significant role in the material dispossession, exploitation and partial eradication of indigenous peoples within each settler colony'.[75] To some settler communities, part of the appeal of Britannic nationalism lay in the possibilities it offered to reinforce racial barriers to migration and belonging, to deny full membership of the nation to indigenous peoples and non-white migrants.[76] Ideas about **otherness** and the production of difference, encountered in Chapter 3, are thus of some relevance here too. As one historian has argued, attempts to exclude Asian migrants provided a particularly powerful motivation for emphasizing British identity across the settler colonies.

> The centrality of whiteness and Britishness, and the occasional conflict between these two identities, in part, depended on an Asian 'other' which captured settler imaginations in the late nineteenth and early twentieth centuries. Indigenous peoples were the others of the early nineteenth century, but each colony had a distinctive 'native problem', whereas Asian migration increasingly became *the* issue which could unite disparate parts of the Anglo-British World.[77]

Yet Britishness could never simply be equated with whiteness or with biological ideas about race. In Britain itself, Britishness had after all emerged as an avowedly non-ethnic identity, a means to unite the diverse peoples of the United Kingdom without replacing their separate identities as members of English, Irish, Scottish, and Welsh nations. Britishness was always a composite identity, based on high culture and shared institutions. In an imperial setting, it thus had a significant capacity to integrate non-British whites, such as the Irish, French Canadians, and Afrikaners.[78] As discussed above, Africans and Asians could also claim to be 'black Englishmen' or 'brown Britons', British subjects who shared British culture and (crucially) political rights, even if those claims were not always heeded.

▶ Conclusions

The British empire was an unstable amalgam of different peoples, assembled at sword-point and yet relying on a wide range of more subtle integrative processes to ensure that coercion was the weapon of last resort rather than an everyday tool of dominance. In this regard, it was probably like most other empires in world history. Historians have paid more attention to resistance, nationalism, and the disintegration of the British empire than they have to the more mundane, but nevertheless crucial, forces of integration that held Britain's world-system together. They have also tended to assume that nationalism and imperialism were starkly oppositional forces, when in fact a great deal of recent work suggests that they were inextricably linked, in some ways locked in combat, but in other ways complementary to one another. We are only just beginning to appreciate how complex was the impact of empire on identities across the globe.

In South Asia, British rule produced a form of Indian political organization concerned more with broadening opportunities for collaboration than with overturning the colonial order and risking a social revolution. It was the inability of the British to move fast or far enough to accommodate these demands, the drastic loss of British resources occasioned by the Second World War, and the growing inability of the British to compel the Indian peasantry to pay the costs associated with deploying the Indian army to fight the wars of empire, that together encouraged British policy-makers to quit India. The fear of communal chaos perhaps loomed larger than the threat of nationalism in speeding up this process of imperial retreat.

In other parts of Asia, and in Africa, colonial rule seemed to produce hybrid communities and forms of identity that long remained compatible with Britain's interests, even if they were not shaped to correspond directly with British demands and influences. Colonial cultures were not entirely antagonistic to British rule, but neither did they necessarily develop in the way that official and non-official agents of empire hoped. The ability of the British to shape the world to suit their requirements was strictly limited.

British identities 'at home' were also influenced by empire, in ways that offered some support to structures and practices of overseas influence. Nevertheless, the imprint of empire on British identity was not straightforward or clearly hegemonic. Empire meant many different things to many different groups and individuals, and was not simply associated with a sense of racial superiority. As it was exported overseas, in the settler colonies of the 'British world' and elsewhere, Britishness adapted and changed to suit a range of disparate agendas. These processes were too diffuse and varied to be controlled to meet the needs of empire in any simple, instrumental fashion.

The 'cultural turn' in historical writing has immeasurably enriched our understanding of the complexity and diversity of identities across the British empire, providing a whole range of case studies that illustrate the subtle and specific consequences of colonial rule and imperial influence in many different places. Yet attempts to offer overarching accounts of the general role of the British empire in shaping identities have seldom proved convincing. The concept of **hegemony**, for example, seems to be too blunt an instrument for understanding the tortuous politics of identity, in Britain and its colonies, and can offer but limited assistance in assembling a meaningful general pattern out of the many examples that historians have made available to us.

This problem is not just a result of the dauntingly broad scope of British imperial history, the difficulties involves in extending any general interpretation to cover all of the places and peoples encompassed by the British empire. It is also a reflection of the nature of cultural history, of the difficulties that cultural historians face in terms of measuring the representativeness of the different individuals or texts that form the basis for their research, and of gauging the relative significance of those examples when compared with other individuals or texts. Sceptical political or economic historians – as we have seen, Bernard Porter is perhaps the extreme example – often complain that the body of evidence contained in cultural histories of empire does not bear the weight of interpretation placed upon it. Cultural history is good at bringing out complexity, but perhaps not so suited to assembling convincing overarching interpretive structures. The next chapter considers recent attempts to write 'global histories' of empire: some would argue that these can help us understand the big picture, the general patterns operating across the broad sweep of the imperial past, but at the cost of obscuring its complexities and varieties.

5 Going Global

▶ Empire and the origins of global history

In 1998 it seemed to John Comaroff that Marxist accounts that had traditionally presented imperialism as 'a reflex of the global expansion of capitalism, of the articulation of modes of production, of unequal exchange between centres and peripheries, of underdevelopment and dependency' had been superseded. Few historians still identified themselves as Marxists, and many former Marxists had turned (with remarkable speed) to postmodern and **postcolonial** ways of thinking to provide a new and very different theoretical underpinning to their work.[1] Yet this obituary was in some ways premature.

Marx himself had paid little attention to empire, but did hint that British (and European) expansion was a crucial engine of historical change, the means by which a 'world market' for capitalism might emerge. Marx was a contemporary observer of the world that was being made by British free-trade imperialism, as it assembled ever-larger markets for capitalist exploitation. While later Marxist thinkers would lament the violence of this process, Marx himself 'noted without regret the destruction of outdated economic and social systems as a necessary stage towards bourgeois and eventually communist society'. The British *raj* in India was, he thought, destroying unprogressive Indian regimes, ushering India into the capitalist age, and hastening the path towards bourgeois and ultimately proletarian dominance. 'The extension of capitalism to hitherto undeveloped parts of the world seemed to him ultimately beneficial to humanity, however much human suffering it might cause.'[2]

During the late 1960s, more critical accounts of this process emerged, labelled 'dependency theory' and 'world systems theory'. Writers such as Andre Gunder Frank and Immanuel Wallerstein argued that the industrialization and imperialism of the European and North American **core** had actively impoverished the African, Asian, and South American **periphery**. The unequal world economic order of today was not the result of pre-existing disparities (the 'West' simply using its superior natural and human resources to overtake the 'rest') but was the result of the systematic 'underdevelopment' of the **periphery** by the **core** during the modern period.[3]

Although neither these theories nor more avowedly Marxist interpretations are likely to dominate the study of imperial history any time soon, 'global' histories of empire now seem to be in the ascendant. These histories are certainly concerned with some of the same issues as earlier Marxist accounts: the 'global expansion of capital'; economic exchanges and connections between imperial powers and their colonies (as well as wider patterns of global interconnection); and questions about the historic roots of disparities and inequalities between different parts of the world. Perhaps the most influential recent work in this regard has been Kenneth Pomeranz's book, *The Great Divergence*. In a wide-ranging and subtle analysis, Pomeranz compares the economies of Europe, China, and Japan, focusing on the eighteenth century. He argues that while much of Europe's economic growth in this period was internally generated, overseas expansion represented one of the crucial sources of the accelerating gap between European and Asian economies. Expansion in the New World, and particularly the development of the plantation and slave systems of the Americas, provided Europe with a key means to escape limits placed on growth by the scarcity of land. Colonization offered Europe a huge new area in which to grow food, plant fibres, and timber, allowing economic activity back in the metropole to focus on manufacturing. For Pomeranz, Europe's leap into industrialization was made possible by the creation of a 'new kind of periphery' in the New World. Slave plantations in the Americas provided Britain with a means to intensify and expand production of primary materials overseas. Slavery also created markets which were particularly dependent on imports of British products, as the slave colonies produced few subsistence goods, and had to import substantial amounts of food and manufactures. The nineteenth-century divergence between Europe and Asia in terms of economic growth was thus, according to Pomeranz, a product of 'the fruits of overseas coercion'.[4]

Many historians now recognize that the history of the British empire was closely intertwined with the increasing economic connectedness of many parts of the world. British imperial expansion occurred at the same time as a single global market for goods, capital, credit, and financial services began to emerge. As we have seen in the preceding chapters, information, knowledge, ideas, and culture also flowed across the internal boundaries of the British empire.[5] Increasing amounts of news were transmitted around the British empire in the late nineteenth and early twentieth centuries, and reports could travel more quickly than ever before. This was encouraged by the broader commercial and personal connections that linked the different parts of the British empire, but was also constrained by the empire's monopolistic media structures and geopolitical requirements.[6] Long-distance migration offered further evidence that the empire was part of an increasingly interconnected world. Large numbers of British and Irish people moving to the 'settler' colonies (and to the United

States). Many Asian and African migrants, free and unfree, also following imperial paths to global mobility. As historians have pointed out, British imperial
expansion was also intertwined with environmental change on a global scale,
notably through the movement around the world of scientists, scientific
knowledge, and animal and plant specimens. Such global movements facilitated the exploitation and management of natural resources, such as forests,
and the introduction of alien crops and livestock to ecosystems in Britain and
in the colonies, sometimes with devastating results.[7]

The growth of global history as a vibrant new sub-field over the last 15 years
reflects a range of influences. Widespread public interest in **globalization** has
set the agenda for historians interested in writing 'usable pasts' that speak to
contemporary concerns. Our world seems to be becoming ever more densely
interconnected, different places linked with each other in a variety of ways,
and often across vast distances. At the same time, the authority of the nation-
state seems to some extent to be weakening. The clear national boundaries
established during the nineteenth and early twentieth centuries have been frac-
tured by political devolution and fragmentation, and blurred by the creation
of international structures such as the European Union. Transnational corpora-
tions now appear to be more powerful than some national governments. Flows
of migrants have encouraged governments to adopt policies of multicultural-
ism, complicating earlier ideas about the link between ethnicity and national
belonging. Historians have been quick to respond to these changes:

> For the moment at least, writing the history of nations and states seems much
> less important than tracing the origins of our world of movement, with its fre-
> netic exchange of goods and ideas, its hybrid cultures and its fluid identities.
> A new global history has grown up in response. Its units of study are regions
> or oceans, long-distance trades, networks of merchants, the tracks of wandering
> scholars, the traffic of cults and beliefs between cultures and continents.[8]

Global history offers us the opportunity to put state structures, national identities, and exercises in nation-building in the context of transnational forces and
processes. It also allows us to correct accounts written by social scientists that
have exaggerated the novelty of **globalization**. Historians have sought to
demonstrate that processes of global integration are not entirely new phenomena: that the world is not 'ten years old', despite what one simplifying pundit
would have us believe.[9]

Imperial historians have played a particularly prominent part in the writing
of the new global history. There are a number of reasons for this. First, global
history seems to offer a way to 'put Humpty-Dumpty back together again'.
In the 1970s and 1980s, imperial history seemed to disintegrate as a field, as

historians moved towards writing national histories and Area Studies that showed little interest in empires as overarching structures of rule.[10] For global historians, by contrast, empires are exactly the sort of large-scale systems that can help us explore how different places and peoples were connected together over time. Second, global history has generally allotted economic history a central place in scholarship. This has offered a lifeline to imperial historians interested in what had become, in the wake of the cultural turn, a deeply unfashionable field. Finally, and perhaps most controversially, we might see the move towards writing global history as part of a broader backlash against the cultural turn. Global historians are not necessarily uninterested in cultural history, and some of the **new imperial history** is implicitly and explicitly global in its scope. Nevertheless, for some imperial historians, global history has offered a way of moving beyond the cultural turn and away from **postcolonial** and postmodern theories and perspectives. It has put grand political and economic narratives, scorned by many postmodern writers, back at the centre of history writing.[11]

Whatever their motives, imperial historians have made significant advances in showing how complex, globe-spanning connections and reciprocal flows of influence linked together and shaped the disparate parts of the British empire. Yet one of the key questions arising out of this work concerns the precise nature of the relationship between empire and **globalization**. For some historians, the British empire was itself an active agent of **globalization**, with policy-makers more-or-less consciously pioneering the creation of a more densely inter-connected world. For others, the British empire is best represented as the passive subject of larger globalizing processes which were beyond the control of the British. For a while, these processes conferred upon the British global dominance and formal or informal control over vast swathes of territory. Later, however, the same forces brought national decline and imperial collapse.[12] Thus, according to Jan Nederveen Pieterse, empire is best understood as a mere epiphenomenon, and **globalization** as the more important and enduring historical process. While empire involved attempts by particular states to exert political power, **globalization** is a broader, more amorphous, and hence more powerful process, according to which a whole range of economic actors and forces have sought to create a more interconnected world order. 'Empires come and go, globalization continues.'[13]

This chapter starts by examining some of the large-scale histories of empire and **globalization**, which trace big political and economic processes operating over long stretches of time. It seeks to draw out the connections between these histories and many of the older theories and concepts that have been developed to help explain the history of the British empire. The chapter then goes on to examine histories that develop ideas about webs and networks, and that offer a 'networked' account of British imperial history. This work shares much in common with recent scholarship in the field of **transnational history**. Shifting the scale of analysis, the chapter then looks at how historians have sought to write global and imperial lives, following individuals in their movements around the world. This approach to life-writing can illustrate the manifold, long-distance connections that helped shape and were shaped by the modern British empire.

► Global histories of empire

Global history is a relatively new sub-field, and its boundaries and precise nature are not yet fixed. For some, global history is about large-scale processes, which need to be viewed from an analytical perspective that takes in the whole world, and perhaps also to be understood as operating over a very long period of time. According to this interpretation, the history of British overseas expansion needs to be presented as part of a much broader story of empire-building.

In the 1960s the Swiss historian Herbert Lüthy made an early attempt to outline what such a history might look like. Lüthy argued that historians should write an overarching 'history of colonization'. Rather than focus on what he saw as the extraneous, 'transitory' details of political rule and rivalry, Lüthy argued that this history should chart

> the tremendous process by which the world was discovered, opened to man, and settled; the process by which roads, coasts and oceans were made accessible and safe, by which closed continents, forbidden kingdoms and isolated societies were forced open or broken up by new expanding forces, new techniques, new customs, new knowledge, and new forms of social organization.

For Lüthy, this was a step towards writing a universal 'history of humanity'. Lives everywhere had been influenced by the massive transformations of the previous five centuries, which had reshaped the planet's environment and demography and created a 'world-wide economy'. For Lüthy, this would also be an explicitly unifying history, a usable past to support 'the integration of mankind' at a time when Cold War rivalries threatened the future of humanity.[14]

In keeping with the political purposes of his project, Lüthy thought that historians should not dwell upon the violence and inequalities of the imperial past. Indeed, he argued that 'colonization' had required minimal use of force due to 'the passive capacity of the non-European world to be colonized'. Colonization and European rule had been inevitable but also transitory phenomena, laying the foundations for self-government.

Europe's colonization of the world, as well as all the partial colonizations which preceded it, was neither a chain of crimes nor a chain of beneficence: it was the painful birth of the modern world itself. None of the former colonial peoples remember it with gratitude, for it was alien rule; but none of them wish to turn back the clock, and this is its historical justification.

For Lüthy, the inevitability of colonization meant that moral judgement was unnecessary, even a dangerous distraction. A global history of modern slavery and the slave trade, for example, had to be written as 'a common history in which Europe, Africa, the Muslim world and the West Indies were taking part, as their history *and* ours'.[15]

In its focus on the role of empires in creating a more densely interconnected world economy, and in linking together different regions and peoples, Lüthy's article anticipated some of the key arguments of later global historians. His claims about the economic necessity and inevitability of colonization are not perhaps all that far removed from Niall Ferguson's recent claim that empire was in effect 'globalization with gunboats', the only means available to integrate outlying regions into the world economy.[16] However, in many respects, Lüthy's arguments seem deeply objectionable to many scholars today. In particular, they look suspiciously like an attempt to chart the progressive spread of 'civilization' from Europe to the rest of the world, and to exonerate the West from blame for the horrors of the imperial past. They present Europe as the driving force in the 'history of humanity', reaching out into passive non-European societies, transforming them, and drawing them kicking and screaming into the 'modern' world.

More recent attempts to write large-scale global histories of empire have thus worked hard to avoid Lüthy's **Eurocentric** assumptions, to emphasize the key role played by non-European agents and non-European empires, and to foreground inequalities of wealth and power. As early as 1988, David Washbrook emphasized the importance of building Indian history into any attempt to write transnational or global history. South Asia was central both to early-modern systems of long-distance trade and exchange, and to the long-range connections subsequently built by the British empire in the nineteenth century. Such networks demonstrated that global connections were neither an exclusively modern phenomenon nor simply the result of European industrialization and empire building. Asian merchants, entrepreneurs, and financiers built powerful sets of connections around Asian cities and trade routes, which in the eighteenth century were as formidable as any economic system that centred on Europe. They were an essential part of the history of the modern world economy, which thus cannot be understood simply in terms of the history of Europe.[17] From this perspective, **globalization** might be better understood as the linking up of a range of pre-existing European and non-European long-distance trading systems. Thinking in this way helps us get beyond accounts that see **globalization** as an entirely modern phenomenon, and that focus on Europe and the 'Atlantic World' without considering the sophisticated systems of trade and exchange that traversed the Pacific and Indian oceans.

In *After Tamerlane*, John Darwin has offered a global history of empire from the fifteenth century to the present. For Darwin, empire should be understood as an integral part of a wider global history of commercial and geopolitical connection and contest. Because we live today in a world of nation-states, we tend to think that they are the natural way of organizing the globe. In fact, Darwin argues, nation-states have been the exception, not the rule: empires have been 'the default mode of political organization throughout most of history'.[18] If we neglect this fact, then we miss the key forces shaping much of global history.

Darwin adapts many of the concepts and theories about imperial expansion and contraction that we encountered in Chapter 1, and places them in the context of global history. He traces how different power blocs centred in different parts of the 'Eurasian' landmass (and eventually also in North America) have vied to harness the resources of distant areas in order to create a dominant commercial and strategic position for themselves. When those power blocs succeeded in bringing sufficient economic and military resources under their command, they became empires. During the seventeenth and eighteenth centuries, the European powers drew in the resources of the Americas to build their empires. This facilitated, but did not make inevitable, the subjugation of Asian resources. It was industrialization, but also strong state structures, new military and communications technologies, and Britain's new geopolitical predominance (its victory over France, its maritime superiority, and its possession in India of a springboard into Asia), which together 'opened the road for an imperial order in which European control was riveted on the rest of the globe' during the nineteenth century.[19]

Following in the footsteps of Robinson and Gallagher, Darwin downplays the significance of annexation and direct control in explaining nineteenth-century British dominance. He writes of 'commercial empire' and 'territorial empire', terms analogous to **informal** and **formal empire**. He also agrees with Robinson and Gallagher that annexation and direct control tended to be the weapons of last resort for imperial powers seeking to harness the resources of distant regions. Formal control was the least elegant and most damaging option, the one most likely to prove counter-productive in terms of awakening opposing forces of resistance within the subjugated territory and among rival empires. Darwin sees formal control as the battering ram of empire:

> It could break open markets that resisted free trade, or (as in India) conscript local resources to build the railways and roads that European traders demanded.

It could promise protection to European entrepreneurs, or (as happened often in Africa) make them a free gift of local land and labour. But it also relied on the technological, industrial and financial assets that Europe could deploy.

In order to avoid a **Eurocentric** perspective, and to demonstrate the role played by non-Europeans in the history of empires, Darwin again draws on Robinson and Gallagher, deploying their 'peripheral' approach. He emphasizes that imperial powers seldom had things entirely their own way in their colonies, and were not all-powerful, transformative behemoths. To mobilize the resources they required, they needed to make deals with and concessions to local players, which in turn left room for 'the resilience of many of Eurasia's other states and cultures in the face of Europe's expansion'.[20]

The overall result of the creation of modern empires, Darwin argues, was **globalization**, or at least 'semi-globalization'. Through empire, Europe drew the rest of the world into a new global economy, as producers of food and raw materials, as borrows of European capital, and as consumers of Western industrial goods. Britain and the other European powers were not able to deliver the transformative, world-shaping results that propagandists of the free-trade world order had promised. Perhaps with the exception of India (which faced the full onslaught of British economic and military interests under the conditions imposed by direct imperial control), Asian economies often proved far more difficult to penetrate than Western entrepreneurs had initially hoped. For all the shock and awe of gunboat diplomacy, this was the real lesson of European involvement in China. Formidable practical obstacles to Western enterprise also remained throughout tropical Africa. Nevertheless, the result of European commercial and territorial empire was the breakdown of old regional commercial structures, and the creation of a 'vast semi-unified system of economics and politics, a common area from which no state, society, economy or culture was able to remain entirely aloof'. This system was only destroyed by the slide of the European state system into war in 1914, another indicator of Europe's imperfect ability to shape the world to its will and perhaps proof that Europe did not possess the key to creating stable state structures after all. Under the combined shocks of the Great Depression of the 1930s, the Second World War, and the Cold War, globalizing processes subsequently went 'into sharp reverse'. **Decolonization** meant the undoing of European territorial empires, the waning of European attempts to shape the international order in more subtle ways, and the erosion of European commercial empires. The way was cleared for US dominance, and for the resumption of globalizing processes under American auspices. With its extensive commercial empire, the contemporary US should, Darwin argues, be viewed as an imperial power – indeed, as today's only world empire – even if it does not openly admit to engaging in colonial rule.[21]

An alternative global history of empire has been offered by Christopher Bayly, as part of his wider global history of the long nineteenth century. His account moves even further away from Eurocentrism. In *The Birth of the Modern World*, Bayly argues that global change was 'multi-centric', driven not just by impulses generated in Europe and North America, but by forces emanating from Asia and Africa too. The West may have enjoyed a dominant position in the nineteenth century, projecting its power overseas through a range of imperial influences, but that dominance was neither complete nor uncontested. The growth of a more formidable form of state structure in Europe, capable of mobilizing the resources of its subjects, and deploying them in militarily effective ways against its rivals, provides for Bayly the key to understanding the Western lead in this period. Other forces – industrialization, improvements in communications, ideologies of superiority and rule – played an important but supplementary role. The differences between the 'West' and the 'rest' were ones of degree, not absolutes. Indeed, Bayly attempts to show the common ground upon which we can base a global history in which eighteenth- and twentieth-century convergence bookend the nineteenth-century 'great divergence' between Europe and Asia. This in turn allows us to see that divergence in its longer-term historical context, as something both unusual and temporary.[22]

▶ Networked histories of empire

Other global historians of empire are less interested in large-scale processes or very long time-frames. Instead, they see global history as a way of writing detailed histories of interconnection, concerned with the various ties that bound together specific places and people at particular times. These scholars have much in common with those working in the field of **transnational history** and focusing on the past 'interaction and circulation of ideas, peoples, institutions or technologies' over long distances.[23] **Transnational history** tends to be concerned with the 'connectors' that provided concrete links between different places and peoples.[24] Yet it can be difficult to fit imperial history into the context of **transnational history**, for the simple reason that studying empires often involves examining territorial units that cannot be described as nations without risking serious anachronism. Moreover, in empires, **core** and **periphery** are bound together in distinctive and highly unequal ways: these links cannot easily be subsumed into more general (and possibly more benign) accounts of transnational interconnection.

Much recent work in imperial history has built on ideas about global webs and networks. This has to some extent been inspired by the writings of social scientists, who have emphasized the importance of transnational networks covering large spaces, networks that reinforced and reshaped existing social, cultural, political, and economic relationships.[25] Tony Ballantyne is notable among those imperial historians who have used the idea of webs to help explain the various connections that linked Britain with its colonies, that bound colonies up with other colonies, and that connected them with places beyond the boundaries of the British empire. For Ballantyne, thinking about these webs moves us away from the traditional, binary model of empire that focuses on the relationship between **core** and **periphery**, and instead encourages us to consider complex flows of human, intellectual, and material traffic that moved in all sorts of directions. In his study of how racial theories of Aryanism were deployed in different parts of the British empire, Ballantyne shows how webs of interconnection were used both to justify the colonial order and to subvert colonial knowledge (see Chapter 2) and structures of dominance. Print culture, and particularly the press, provided the key medium through which ideas about race and empire could travel around the globe and be retooled for different purposes. Webs drew together people and places, gave some 'nodes' particular local or transnational significance, and were 'constantly reworked and remade' as they were adapted to new conditions and requirements. These webs of empire were, according to Ballantyne, 'powerful agents of globalization'.

> The imperial globalization generated by British commerce, conquest and colonization had two important effects. Firstly, and most obviously, imperial networks brought previously unconnected regions together into a system, albeit a highly uneven one, of exchange and movement. Secondly, it transformed worldviews: globalization was (and is) as much a state of mind as a series of capital flows or migratory movements. The British empire transformed the ways in which people, both in Britain and in the colonies, thought about the world. [26]

Alan Lester has similarly emphasized the importance of what he labels 'imperial networks', which carried flows of goods, people, and ideas, and which shaped Britain as much as they did its colonies. Lester's own work focuses on two sets of connections: those formed by humanitarians campaigning against the ill-treatment of indigenous peoples around the mid-nineteenth-century British empire; and those constructed by settlers in response to these humanitarian attacks. Looking at these two groups in the Cape Colony, New South Wales, and New Zealand, Lester shows how humanitarians and settlers competed to convince British policy-makers and the British public of the truth of their own versions of events on the frontier of settlement. Both humanitarians and settlers sought to gather individual cases and incidents together into a broader argument. This involved creating networks of communication, to draw together evidence from around the empire and to transmit it to audiences in Britain and in other colonies.

The resulting, competing imperial networks carried ideas and information around the empire. In an age before the telegraph, reports were carried by messengers, letters, and newspapers, aboard ship and over land. For Lester, these networks had several significant effects. While humanitarians made the case that all people should be protected by the law, regardless of race, settlers argued that indigenous peoples were irredeemably inferior, given over to savage outbursts of violence, and had to be treated accordingly. Coercion and dispossession were thus justified, and indigenous peoples became the 'other' against which settler versions of Britishness were defined. Settler networks also helped create a global sense of British identity. Humanitarians argued that, through their violent treatment of indigenous peoples, settlers had departed from British traditions of justice. Settlers countered that they remained British, tied to a broad racial community of fellow-Britons in the colonies and at home, and retaining the right to metropolitan support in their dealings with non-Europeans. Their arguments in turn helped reshape ideas about Britishness in Britain itself.[27]

Like Ballantyne, Lester has argued that this networked conception of empire is of broader applicability. He emphasizes that 'concepts such as networks, webs and circuits ... [allow the] histories of Britain and its colonies to be conceived as more fluidly and reciprocally interrelated,' and are 'very fruitful if one wants to consider metropole and colony, or colony and colony, within the same analytical frame, and without necessarily privileging either one'.[28] In some ways, these arguments (which question the utility of the traditional distinction drawn by historians between the categories of **core** and **periphery**) echo the earlier insights of Ronald Robinson. Robinson similarly focused attention on the complex, back-and-forth flow of influences and inputs between Britain and its colonies: 'when imperialism is looked at as an inter-continental process, its true metropolis appears neither at the centre nor on the periphery, but in their changing relativities'.[29]

Historians of the 'British world' (a concept discussed above in Chapter 4), have also drawn on the idea of imperial networks. Kent Fedorowich and Andrew Thompson argue that the British world was constituted of 'a series of interlocking networks, webs and information flows, which ranged from family and community affiliations, to commercial, scientific and professional bodies, to educational, philanthropic, religious and labour groups'.[30] Writing with Gary Magee, Thompson has suggested that British migration was accompanied by the creation of 'trans-national networks', binding the British diaspora together and shaping the nature of British overseas economic engagement. Imperial networks encouraged Britons at home to trade with Britons overseas, and also limited commercial engagement with other places.[31] Tamson Pietsch suggests that we should think in terms of multiple British worlds, of competing and coexisting networks and shifting sets of interconnection that bound different groups of people together in many and varied ways.[32]

Part of the appeal of a networked approach derives from its compatibility with the **new imperial history**. Both can involve an emphasis on mutual connections between **metropole** and colony, and on connections among different sites of colonization. A networked approach offers a way to 'decentre' Britain, to shift emphasis away from the imperial **core**. However, it would be wrong to see networked histories of empire as some sort of panacea, curing all the ills of past accounts. For if we place too much emphasis on fluid, ephemeral, reciprocal networks, we can end up writing histories that emphasize negotiation and exchange at the expense of accounting for fundamental inequalities of power. Networks were themselves bound up in these inequalities, and while they may have offered opportunities to subvert and resist imperial and colonial power, they were also used by officials, business interests, and other agents of empire to maintain their dominance.[33] We can also exaggerate the significance of the links that connected different colonies to one another, and thus run the risk of underestimating the continued importance of the fundamental imperial bond between Britain and each of its colonies. London remained the hub of most imperial networks. The links that connected colony to colony were generally sparser and weaker than the links between **core** and **periphery**.[34] In the world of broadcasting, for example, twentieth-century imperial connections were dominated by a small number of large institutions, and most notably by the British Broadcasting Corporation operating out of London. These connections displayed few of the qualities of a flexible, mobile, fluid network: they were strong, but highly organized and relatively static. Close connections were maintained between the BBC and broadcasting authorities in Canada, Australia, and New Zealand, but links with broadcasters in Africa and Asia were always noticeably weaker.[35]

Indeed, we should acknowledge that in the 'semi-globalized' world order associated with the British empire, some places simply did not get networked, or at least were connected up much less frequently. As Frederick Cooper argues,

> The world has long been – and still is – a space where economic and political relations are very uneven; it is filled with lumps, places where power coalesces surrounded by those where it does not, places where social relations become dense amid others that are diffuse. Structures and networks penetrate certain places and do certain things with great intensity, but their effects tail off elsewhere.[36]

The 'semi-globalization' of the nineteenth and twentieth centuries failed to reach many parts of tropical Africa and Asia. Forces of global integration similarly seemed to bypass Britain's older colonies in the Caribbean.[37] It might be argued, that in this respect, the limits of twenty-first century **globalization** have deep historical roots: or, following Cooper, we might conclude that **globalization** is simply a vague catch-all term that is not particularly helpful when trying to explain specific, limited, and partial patterns of past and contemporary long-distance interconnection.[38] What is for certain is that any networked account of British imperial history is bound to be incomplete if it fails to account for agglomerations of power in certain places and among certain people, and for the gaps that limited the extent and potency of webs of global interconnection.[39]

▶ Imperial and global lives

Another approach to integrating imperial history and global history has involved examining the lives of individuals who engaged in long-distance travel, voluntarily or involuntarily, and who crossed the British empire's territorial and cultural boundaries in the process.

Linda Colley's book *Captives* represented a pioneering attempt to combine 'the large-scale, panoramic and global, with the small-scale, the individual, and the particular', through the captivity narratives of British and Irish men and women from the early seventeenth to the mid-nineteenth century. In relating these life stories, Colley demonstrated how they reflected 'both the growing scale of Britain's global reach and its persistent limitations'.[40] Her subsequent book, *The Ordeal of Elizabeth Marsh*, examined one of these life stories in even greater detail, looking at how one woman's life was shaped by mid-eighteenth-century processes of global change: 'a world in a life and a life in the world'. Marsh experienced 'some of the main forces of global change of her time: enhanced maritime reach, transoceanic and transcontinental commerce, a more deliberate mobilization of knowledge and written information in the service of the state, the quickening tempo of imperial aggression and colonization, emigration, war, slavery and the slave trade'.[41]

As Colley argues, one of the advantages of this approach to global history, employing the techniques of life-writing, is that it helps return a human dimension to our understanding of otherwise-impersonal global forces of change.[42] Following much the same vein, Emma Rothschild has piecing together the eighteenth-century lives of members of one family and 'their households, friends, servants, and slaves'. She looks at how 'information and expectations' connected individuals and groups across different sites of colonization. For Rothschild, this is about showing how we can write 'microhistories' of individuals and families that cover wide areas of the globe, and tackle large-scale processes of global historical change. As Rothschild points out, we also need to factor 'disconnections or discontinuities' into such microhistories. **Globalization** was never total.[43]

David Lambert and Alan Lester have sought to shed further light on such global lives by suggesting that we examine the 'imperial careers' of people who lived and worked in multiple sites of empire.

> Within each of the colonies they inhabited, these people had opportunities to transcend their initial impressions, to insinuate themselves into personal, business, official, religious and friendship networks ... their life histories – indeed, their life geographies – constituted meaningful connections across the empire in their own right. And these connections were one kind among many which facilitated the continual reformulation of imperial discourses, practices and culture. [44]

Such imperial careers helped create and strengthen networks of interconnection. It was not just the privileged white elite that experienced global mobility in this period. As we saw in the previous chapter, the nineteenth and twentieth centuries also saw unprecedented numbers of white working-class people leave Britain and Ireland and engage in global mobility. Examining this white diaspora might help us write global history 'from below'. As Fedorowich and Thompson argue, 'migration made transnationalism – by which we mean living in and identifying with more than one country or place at once – a normal way of life for many British people in the second half of the nineteenth and first half of the twentieth century', encouraging them to see themselves as 'part of a global chain of kith and kin'.[45] Robert Bickers has looked at the possibilities and problems that empire opened up for one 'ordinary' British man working in the Shanghai Municipal Police, simultaneously mobilized and trapped by 'the web of world empire'.[46] Clare Anderson has meanwhile married life-writing techniques with ideas drawn from the Subaltern Studies school of Indian history, to look at the experiences of non-white men and women transported to Britain's penal colonies in the Indian Ocean during the nineteenth century. Anderson's book seeks to reconstruct this convict experience from the scanty fragments that survive in the archival record.[47]

One of the virtues of studying the global mobility of individuals is that it offers a fresh way of analysing the connections that linked the different European (and non-European) empires. British imperial historians have not always been good at thinking about other empires, about comparisons and contrasts between the British empire and other empires, and the ways in which the world's many imperial systems were interlinked. Paradoxically, perhaps, global historians have sometimes suffered from a similar myopia. Much 'global' history is still written in the context of an Anglophone academic world that places undue emphasis on Britain and the British empire, the United States, and other English-speaking places, and that is much less aware of histories that require knowledge of other European and non-European languages and settings. Arguably, if we really want to understand the global impact of the British empire, the extent to which it shaped the political, economic, social, and cultural history of different places, and whether it had a specific and decisively transformative influence, then we need to compare examples from the British empire with ones drawn from other empires, and indeed from regions that were not meaningfully bound into empires. By studying individuals who crossed the boundaries between empires, and between empires and nations, we can make a start on this formidable task. Such individuals were 'connectors', and in their life-histories we might hope to discover the outlines of broader patterns of imperial and global interconnection. Writing 'connected histories' of empire involves combining insights from imperial, global, networked, and transnational histories, exploring the links that joined together Britain and its colonies, but also those that connected different colonies up with one another, and that bonded different parts of the British empire to the metropoles and colonies of other European and non-European empires.[48]

▶ Conclusions

By putting individuals back into global history in these different ways, imperial historians have insisted on the importance of individual **agency** and decision-making. They have restored an element of chance, choice, and contingency to accounts of past **globalization**, and reminded us of the costs as well as the benefits of global mobility. This is important, given the pointed criticisms that have been levelled at types of global history that fail to do this, and that suggest or imply that **globalization** is essentially an unintentional and inevitable outcome of human activity. If we write histories that lack human **agency**, then we are unable to attribute responsibility for past actions to individuals and groups. If the British empire is seen as an inadvertently globalizing force, creating a more densely interconnected world almost by accident, then we are left repeating J. R. Seeley's famous epigram: that the British 'conquered half the world in a fit of absence of mind'.[49] Did agents of British influence and power also connect up half the globe in a similarly distracted state?

Integration into the global economy had damaging and disruptive effects on African and Asian economies and societies. We cannot simply portray empire as a benign state-building process that eventually left colonies ready for economic development, the promises of trusteeship finally fulfilled. As we have seen, in India for example, the British *raj* hardly built the foundations for a 'modern' economy: instead, it 'traditionalized' and 'peasantized' much of Indian society. We might argue that integration into the global economy also caused disruption in Britain and other parts of Europe. Here, however, the damage caused was generally short-lived. In parts of Asia and Africa, the negative effects lasted much longer. Mike Davis argues that the economic crises and famines of the late nineteenth-century colonial world helped shape enduring inequalities between different parts of the globe, the consequences of which can still be observed today. The restructuring of household and regional economies to fit with the requirements of the global market led to short-term disruption, impoverishment, and starvation, and over the long term contributed to a massive erosion of *per capita* incomes. Davis argues that the Western powers took an active, purposeful role in shaping this outcome: 'every serious attempt by a non-Western society to move over into a fast lane of development or to regulate its terms of trade was met by a military as well as an economic response from London or a competing imperial capital'. India, Davis argues, provided a clear example of the deleterious effects of integration into the world economy through empire. The substitution of food security for export-oriented agriculture, the burden of massive military spending, and currency policies designed to benefit Britain rather than India, together meant that India's *per capita* income failed to increase between 1757 and 1947. Between 1872 and 1921, average Indian life expectancy fell by 20 per cent.[50] Although the data upon which these specific claims are based might be open to question, it is impossible to deny that British and wider European empire-building contributed to 'a massive and historic redistribution of the world's resources'.[51]

While imperial history might thus offer examples of the damage that **globalization** can cause, the shift towards global history should remind imperial historians that empire was never the whole story, in terms of Britain's engagement with the world beyond its shores. The recent rediscovery of empire by cultural historians has in particular threatened to inflate and thus distort our understanding of the relative significance of imperial expansion to Britain's own development. Earlier concepts and theories offered a more nuanced understanding of the manifold ways in which Britain engaged with the world beyond its shores. One of the real virtues of the idea of **informal empire**, for example, lies in its ability to bring to our attention the sheer diversity of the various economic (and cultural) connections that linked Britain to the wider world. **Formal empire** was, as Robinson and Gallagher pointed out, only the tip of the iceberg: many other complex sets of informal economic and political arrangements also allowed Britain to exercise power and influence across the globe. Moreover, British people invested in, traded with, and migrated to the United States and other parts of the New World that sat outside

Britain's formal and informal empires. Britain was also intimately connected with many parts of the Old World of Europe. British overseas economic activity was never confined to imperial boundaries, and empire migration, trade, and investment were almost always the minor themes in this wider movement. Global history and imperial history are not synonymous, and should not be treated as such. The empire was not the world.

Similarly, we should not assume that the story of **globalization** is the only, or indeed the dominant, narrative in imperial history. There is a broader danger of anachronism in much global history writing, stemming from the assumption that because we are today often obsessed with the consequences of living in an increasingly interconnected world, then people in the past must likewise have been preoccupied with similar changes going on around them. In reality, in the nineteenth and twentieth centuries 'transnationalism', easy mobility, and convenient and rapid long-distance communication were experienced by only a small percentage of the world's population.[52] Global history adds a significant new element to the study of empires, but it cannot replace imperial history in all its varied forms.

Conclusions

Theory is not something that historians should simply apply in order to slot a topic neatly and uncritically into a broader interpretative framework, or to confirm the wisdom of a revered canonical thinker or select group of colleagues. Historians should always seek to test the limits of different concepts and theories, to see where they might apply and where they do not. Much of the historiographical debate generated by different theories of empire has revolved around how those theories relate to particular examples and case studies. Whenever a historian claims that a theory must have more general validity because it fits his or her particular case study, then others are quick to counter-attack, and point out the myriad ways in which that theory does not suit their own particular fields of expertise. As we have seen, some of the resulting debates are intractable, even interminable. They sometimes seem to revolve around bafflingly minor differences of emphasis and interpretation. Yet upon such discrepancies theories can stand or fall.

The British empire occupies a central place in the history of the modern world. In many parts of Africa, Asia, the Pacific, and the Americas, and in Britain itself, historians who write insular, hermetically sealed 'national' histories ignore the imperial past at their peril. **Formal empire** bequeathed substantial political, economic, social, and cultural legacies in many different countries. If we take **informal empire** into account, then the impact of the British empire was wider still. The concepts and theories that have been discussed in this book are thus of relevance beyond the disciplinary boundaries of imperial history, narrowly defined, and in some ways should be a common currency for all sorts of historians. For students of international relations and trade, state power, nationalism and identity, migration, race, gender, and globalization, the ideas advanced by imperial historians to make sense of their diverse field are of critical importance.

Studying the development of these ideas also helps us understand how changing approaches to political, economic, social, and cultural history have continued to reshape the writing of history over time, and how different generations of historians have sought to provide their readers with a 'usable past'. In its earliest incarnation, imperial history offered ideological underpinnings for the expansion and maintenance of Britain's overseas empire. In the early twentieth century, some contemporaries then reinterpreted imperial history so as to support a critique of inequalities at home and abroad, and a programme for political action. After the Second World War, imperial history was rewritten partly in the light of new evidence, but also to help make sense of the unfolding reality of **decolonization** and of enduring economic disparities between different parts of the globe. Historians drew parallels between Britain's imperial past and contemporary American economic and cultural expansion and military entanglement in Vietnam and other Cold War conflict zones. Historians also looked to empire to help explain contemporary attitudes to race and inequality at home in Britain. In the early twenty-first century, imperial history again seemed highly relevant in the context of American and British policy in Afghanistan and Iraq. The changing balance of world economic power may, in the future, similarly lead us to rethink the long-term effects and significance of empire. In particular, growing Chinese influence in the world may encourage us to think more deeply about **informal empire**, and other key concepts in imperial history, over the decades to come.

To some extent, two distinct approaches to writing British imperial history have emerged, each deploying its own theoretical and conceptual apparatus. Building on the insights of Ronald Robinson and John Gallagher, the older tradition of imperial history has focused on the metropolitan diplomacy, geopolitics, policy-making, and economics of British overseas expansion, but has also insisted on the importance of the **periphery** in shaping the nature of empire. Particularly in its 'Cambridge school' variant, this tradition has traced how empire was experienced in very different ways from place to place, depending not just on the policies of the metropolitan government and the resources dedicated to establishing colonial bridgeheads by British agents, but also on the nature of existing, pre-colonial polities, economies, societies, and cultures. Now, it seems that this tradition of imperial history might blend into the new surroundings of global history, and perhaps even cease to function as a separate sub-discipline. As argued at the end of Chapter 5, there are several reasons why we should be worried by this prospective merger and what we might lose as a result of it.

The **new imperial history** has meanwhile tended to focus on social and particularly cultural history, inspired by thinkers such as Michel Foucault and Edward Said and engaging with theoretical, interdisciplinary debates generated by the rise of **postcolonialism**. In the process, due to a range of philosophical and political beliefs about how history should be written and what sorts of issues can be approached with confidence, the **new imperial history** has effectively disengaged from some of the key questions that have absorbed political and economic historians. It has instead asked very different sorts of questions and examined very different topics and bodies of evidence, focusing on the attitudes, discourses, and mentalities that accompanied imperial expansion. Paradoxically, perhaps, the **new imperial history** has often shed more light on the history of Britain itself (and particularly the history of British national identity and British attitudes to race and gender difference) than on the structures of day-to-day power and authority that sustained colonial rule in Britain's colonies.

Some practitioners of the **new imperial history** have accused other scholars of neglecting the key dimensions of race, class, and gender, of downplaying the violence and inequality that accompanied imperial expansion and colonial rule, and even of engaging in some form of nostalgic longing for a rose-tinted lost world in which most of the map was painted British imperial pink. Meanwhile, those who have followed in the footsteps of Robinson and Gallagher have often scorned the **new imperial history** as abstractly and misleadingly theoretical and fundamentally mistaken in terms of its view of the priorities for scholarship. These attitudes are not very helpful. They imply that the different approaches to writing imperial history, the various theories and concepts used by historians, are simply alternatives to one another. They imply that one approach is right and the other must be wrong, and that students of imperial history need to decide between the two, on the grounds either of evidence or contemporary political sympathy and conviction.

Yet, as this book has sought to illustrate, in many ways the two most prominent approaches to writing imperial history are complementary. Key concepts in imperial history have, since the 1950s, enjoyed remarkable longevity. Newer theories have tended to coexist side by side with older ones, rather than render them obsolete. This is partly because historical research is often, at heart, a process of collaboration across the generations, with new contributions revising and expanding upon earlier work. Political and economic histories of empire, some of them well-established, have thus tended to form the unacknowledged spine along which social and cultural histories have been arranged and upon which they depend for much of their coherence. The cultural turn may have added a great deal of subtlety and complexity to our understanding of the imperial past, and have allowed us to engage with many new aspects of the history of empire. Yet this has sometimes been achieved at the expense of obscuring the wider patterns, structures, and narratives that political and economic history has been so good at providing.

Meanwhile, the better recent political and economic histories of empire have proved adept at working insights from the field of cultural history into their analysis. Indeed, if the current turn to global history is going to bring any real advance in our understanding of the imperial past, this will not be achieved by tossing cultural histories of empire into the dustbin. Global history offers a fresh and exciting set of perspectives on the history of the British empire, but it is not a replacement for the variety and complexity of British imperial history as it has developed since the 1950s. We need global histories that are alive to the social, cultural, and individual elements of the imperial experience. Global histories should not fold the imperial past into some sort of celebratory, Olympian narrative that recounts the inevitable emergence of an increasingly interconnected world. In the 1980s Ronald Robinson worried that he had started his career 'by criticising histories of empires with rulers without subjects and ended by writing an imperial history with subjects, but without rulers'.[1] We must avoid producing a global history which lacks either, which has structures but not individuals. Global histories need to bring out the damage that the British empire did as well as what some now see as its positive achievements, what it transformed but also what it failed to change, the role it played in perpetuating inequality and difference, the importance of human **agency** and choice, and the ever-present elements of contingency and chance. This would be a really usable past.

Glossary

agency – the ability to make decisions, interact with others, and thus shape the course of events.

collaboration – the active participation of groups of non-Europeans in the running of the colonial state.

communalism – loyalties based on ethnic, linguistic, or religious communities, rather than a sense of national identity, and often generating violent antagonisms between different groups.

core – the coordinating territory at the centre of an imperial system of world influence; the imperial power itself. See also **metropole**.

decolonization – minimally, the ending of formal colonial rule. However, the term may also connote the termination of broader structures of formal and informal political and economic control, the ending of the flow of white settlers to the colonies (and, in some cases, their repatriation), and the transformation of the wider cultural relationship between **core** and **periphery**.

Eurocentric – concepts or theories that attribute all active **agency** to European actors, or that assume that European patterns can simply be applied to the history of other parts of the world.

formal empire – territories that are constitutionally part of the empire; colonies, dependencies, protectorates. Contrast with **informal empire**.

geopolitics – the practice of considering world affairs on a very large scale, often emphasizing the role played by a state's geographical position, the nature of its spatial connections with other states, and the role of geographical features and human, natural, and military resources in shaping coexistence and competition among states.

globalization – the creation of a more densely interconnected world order.

hegemony – the dominant order, pervading all aspects of society and culture, that secures the interests and reinforces the position of the ruling elite.

indirect rule – the policy of governing colonies by devolving the administration of routine local matters to 'traditional' indigenous political structures and leaders.

informal empire – notionally independent territories that are in fact so thoroughly dominated in economic terms that they enjoy little real sovereignty. Contrast with **formal empire**.

invented tradition – supposedly ancient and venerable practices or ceremonies, which are in fact recent innovations designed to bolster the authority of the state or a particular group.

metropole – another name for the **core** territory of an empire.

modernist theories of nationalism – theories which present nationalism as a strictly modern phenomenon, the product of broader changes such as industrialization, urbanization, the growing power of the state, and the development of the modern mass media. Such theories also present the nation as the product of nationalism, rather than *vice versa*.

neocolonialism – the maintenance of the substance of imperial and colonial economic and political influence under the guise of independence.

new imperial history – a wide and diverse body of scholarship, generally marked by its focus on cultural history; its engagement with **postcolonial** theoretical agendas; its interest in divisions of race, class, and gender; and its insistence that Britain itself was fundamentally shaped by the imperial experience.

official mind – politicians and civil servants working collectively, according to shared assumptions, principles, and prejudices, to shape policy according to perceived national interests.

othering – the process of defining one's own identity in opposition to the perceived or constructed attributes of an 'other'.

periphery – the array of formal colonies and territories of informal imperial influence linked to an imperial **core**.

postcolonialism – a set of approaches and perspectives that together seek to reveal all past aspects of the unequal relationship between imperial powers and the rest of the world, particular cultural aspects, as a means ultimately to eliminate those inequalities in the present.

sepoys – Indian soldiers employed by the British for service in India and overseas.

subalterns – groups in society that have been rendered subordinate to the interests of ruling elites.

sub-imperialism – the annexation of new territory, or the expansion of existing colonial frontiers, through the actions of colonial administrators or white settlers 'on the spot'.

transnational history – the study of past movements of people, cultural influences, technologies, etc. over long distances, and primarily across national borders.

Notes

▶ **Introduction**

1 W. David McIntyre, 'Clio and Britannia's Lost Dream: Historians and the British Commonwealth of Nations in the First Half of the 20th Century', *Round Table*, 93 (2004), pp. 517–32. Ronald Hyam, 'The Study of Imperial and Commonwealth History at Cambridge, 1881–1981: Founding Fathers and Pioneer Research Students', *Journal of Imperial and Commonwealth History*, 29:3 (Sept. 2001), pp. 75–103. Frederick Madden, 'The Commonwealth, Commonwealth History, and Oxford, 1905–1971', in Frederick Madden and D. K. Fieldhouse (eds), *Oxford and the Idea of Commonwealth: Essays Presented to Sir Edgar Williams* (London & Canberra, 1982), pp. 7–29. Simon J. Potter, 'What Did You Do in the War, Professor? Imperial History and Propaganda, 1939–45', in Robert Blyth and Keith Jeffery (eds), *The British Empire and Its Contested Pasts* (Dublin and Portland, Oregon, 2009), pp. 24–44.

2 David Fieldhouse, 'Can Humpty-Dumpty Be Put Together Again? Imperial History in the 1980s', *Journal of Imperial and Commonwealth History*, 12:2 (Jan. 1984), pp. 9–23.

3 Raphael Samuel, 'What Is Social History?' in Juliet Gardiner (ed.), *What Is History Today?* (Basingstoke, 1988), pp. 42–48.

4 Hugh Cunningham, 'Jingoism in 1877–78', *Victorian Studies*, 14: 4 (Jun. 1971), pp. 429–53. Richard Price, *An Imperial War and the British Working Class: Working-Class Attitudes and Reactions to the Boer War, 1899–1902* (London, 1972). Freda Harcourt, 'Disraeli's Imperialism, 1866–1868: A Question of Timing', *Historical Journal*, 23:1 (Mar. 1980), pp. 87–109.

5 For a survey and celebration of this project see Andrew S. Thompson (ed.), *Writing Imperial Histories* (Manchester, 2013).

6 E. P. Thompson, *The Making of the English Working Class* (London, 1963).

7 For a wide-ranging critique of the approach of Said and his disciples see John M. MacKenzie, *Orientalism: History, Theory and the Arts* (Manchester, 1995).

8 Kathleen Wilson, 'Introduction: Histories, Empires, Modernities', in Kathleen Wilson (ed.), *A New Imperial History: Culture, Identity and Modernity in Britain and the Empire, 1660–1840* (Cambridge, 2004), pp. 1–26, quote at p. 1.

9 Lord Milner to J. L. Garvin, 27 May 1917, J. L. Garvin Papers, Harry Ransom Centre, Austin, Texas.

10 J. C. D. Clark, *Our Shadowed Present: Modernism, Postmodernism and History* (London, 2003), p. 111.

11 Stephen Howe, *Empire: A Very Short Introduction* (Oxford, 2002), pp. 13–15, quote at p. 13.

12 Edward Gibbon Wakefield, *A View of the Art of Colonization* (London, 1849), p. 15.

13 Jürgen Osterhammel, *Colonialism: A Theoretical Overview* (Princeton, 1997), p. 10.

14 Richard Koebner and Helmut Dan Schmidt, *Imperialism: The Story and Significance of a Political Word, 1840–1960* (Cambridge, 1964), pp. xiii, 1–2. The word was in fact in use in English prior to the 1840s: for example, in 1831 the *Morning Post* referred disparagingly to one Brazilian noble as a 'little sprig of Imperialism'. See *Morning Post* (London), 12 July 1831.

15 Karl Marx, 'Der achtzehnte Brumaire des Louis Bonaparte', in *Karl Marx Friedrich Engels Gesamtausgabe* (Berlin, 1985), first series, vol. 11, pp. 96–189, quote at p. 181.

16 Howe, *Empire*, p. 25.

17 Osterhammel, *Colonialism*, pp. 16–17. Although note that, as with the word 'empire', some would question whether 'rule' is really required for 'colonialism' to exist.

18 C. A. Bayly, 'The First Age of Global Imperialism, c.1760–1830', *Journal of Imperial and Commonwealth History*, 26:2 (May 1998), pp. 28–47, quote at p. 28.

19 Jane H. Ohlmeyer, '"Civilizinge of Those Rude Partes": Colonization within Britain and Ireland, 1580s–1640s', in Nicholas Canny (ed.), *The Oxford History of the British Empire* vol. I *The Origins of Empire: British Overseas Enterprise to the Close of the Seventeenth Century* (Oxford, 1998), pp. 124–47. Keith Jeffery (ed.), *'An Irish Empire'? Aspects of Ireland and the British Empire* (Manchester, 1996). Stephen Howe, *Ireland and Empire: Colonial Legacies in Irish History and Culture* (Oxford, 2000).

20 For an introduction to this literature, see Nicholas Canny and Philip Morgan (eds), *The Oxford Handbook of the Atlantic World, c.1450–c.1850* (Oxford, 2011).

21 P. J. Marshall, *The Making and Unmaking of Empires: Britain, India, and America c.1750–1783* (Oxford, 2005), p. 25.

22 Vincent T. Harlow, *The Founding of the Second British Empire, 1763–1793* (London, 1952–64, 2 vols).

23 On China see Robert Bickers, *The Scramble for China: Foreign Devils in the Qing Empire, 1832–1914* (London, 2011).

24 James Belich, *Replenishing the Earth: The Settler Revolution and the Rise of the Anglo-World, 1783–1939* (Oxford, 2009).

25 John Gallagher, *The Decline, Revival and Fall of the British Empire: The Ford Lectures and Other Essays*, Anil Seal (ed.) (Cambridge, 1982).

26 John Darwin, 'A Third British Empire? The Dominion Idea in Imperial Politics', in Judith M. Brown and Wm. Roger Louis (eds), *The Oxford History of the British Empire* vol. IV *The Twentieth Century* (Oxford, 1999), pp. 64–87.

27 Here see Canny (ed.), *Oxford History of the British Empire* vol. I and P. J. Marshall (ed.), *The Oxford History of the British Empire* vol. II *The Eighteenth Century* (Oxford, 1998).

▶ 1 Expansion and Contraction

1 Joseph A. Schumpeter, 'The Sociology of Imperialisms' in R. Swedberg (ed.), *Joseph A. Schumpeter: the Economics and Sociology of Capitalism* (Princeton, 1991) pp. 141–219, quote at p. 163. This essay was first published as two articles in 1918 and 1919.

2 Stephen Howe, *Anticolonialism in British Politics: the Left and the End of Empire, 1918–1964* (Oxford, 1993), p. 3.

3 J. A. Hobson, *Imperialism: A Study* (London, 3rd Edition, 1988 [1938]), pp. 6–13. The first edition was published in 1902.

4 Ibid., pp. 38, 46.

5 Ibid., pp. 46–61, 81–91, quotes at pp. 53–4 and 57.

6 Wolfgang J. Mommsen, *Theories of Imperialism* (London, 1980), pp. 35–47. Norman Etherington, *Theories of Imperialism: War, Conquest and Capital* (London and Canberra, 1984), pp. 109–29.

7 V. I. Lenin, *Imperialism: the Highest Stage of Capitalism* (London, 1993 [1916]).

8 D. K. Fieldhouse, '"Imperialism": an Historiographical Revision', *Economic History Review*, New Series, 14:2 (1961), pp. 187–209, esp. pp. 189–90.

9 Peter Cain, *Hobson and Imperialism: Radicalism, New Liberalism, and Finance 1887–1938* (Oxford, 2002), p. 277. Cain's book contains a full discussion of Hobson's thinking and inspirations.

10 Eric Stokes, 'Late Nineteenth-Century Colonial Expansion and the Attack on the Theory of Economic Imperialism: a Case of Mistaken Identity?', *Historical Journal*, 12:2 (1969), pp. 285–301. Mommsen, *Theories of Imperialism*, p. 47. Etherington, *Theories of Imperialism*, p. 192.

11 W. K. Hancock, *Survey of British Commonwealth Affairs* vol. II *Problems of Economic Policy, 1918–1939*, part 1 (London, 1940), pp. 1–2.

12 D. K. Fieldhouse, *The Theory of Capitalist Imperialism* (London and Harlow, 1967), p. xvi.

13 Ronald Robinson, 'Non-European Foundations of European Imperialism: Sketch for a Theory of Collaboration', pp. 117–42, quote at p. 118, in R. Owen and B. Sutcliffe (eds), *Studies in the Theory of Imperialism* (London, 1972).

14 John Gallagher and Ronald Robinson, 'The Imperialism of Free Trade', *Economic History Review*, second series, 5:1 (1953), pp. 1–15, quote at p. 3.

15 Ibid., quote at p. 6.

16 Ibid., quote at p. 11.

17 Ibid., quote at p. 13.

18 Ibid., quotes at pp. 12, 13.

19 Ronald Robinson and John Gallagher with Alice Denny, *Africa and the Victorians: the Official Mind of Imperialism* (London, 2nd edition, 1981), quotes at pp. 19, 20. The first edition was published in 1961.

20 Ibid., pp. 66, 68, 92, 470.

21 Ibid., p. 464.

22 Ibid., p. 120.

23 Ibid., p. 162.

24 Ibid., p. 461.

25 For debates about Robinson and Gallagher's ideas see Oliver MacDonagh, 'The Anti-Imperialism of Free Trade', *Economic History Review*, second series, 14:3 (1962), pp. 489–501; D. C. M. Platt, 'The Imperialism of Free Trade: Some Reservations', *Economic History* Review, second series, 21:2 (Aug. 1968), pp. 296–306; D. C. M. Platt, 'Further Objections to an "Imperialism of Free Trade", 1830–60', *Economic History Review*, second series, 26:1 (1973), pp. 77–91; Peter Winn, 'British Informal Empire in Uruguay in the Nineteenth Century', *Past & Present*, 73 (Nov. 1976), pp. 100–26; Martin Lynn, 'The "Imperialism of Free Trade" and the Case of West Africa, c.1830–c.1870', *Journal of Imperial and Commonwealth History*, 15:1 (Oct. 1986), pp. 22–40; and Martin Lynn, 'British Policy, Trade, and Informal Empire in the Mid-Nineteenth Century' in Andrew Porter (ed.), *The Oxford History of the British Empire* vol. III *The Nineteenth Century* (Oxford, 1999), pp. 101–21.

26 Fieldhouse, *Theory of Capitalist Imperialism*, p. 190. D. K. Fieldhouse, *Economics and Empire, 1830–1914* (London, 1973), pp. 49–62.

27 Fieldhouse, *Economics and Empire*, p. 155.

28 Ibid., p. 263.

29 Ronald Hyam, 'The Primacy of Geopolitics: the Dynamics of British Imperial Policy, 1763–1963', *Journal of Imperial and Commonwealth History*, 27:2 (May 1999), pp. 27–52, quote at p. 28.

30 Quoted in ibid., p. 31.

31 Ibid., p. 46.

32 D. K. Fieldhouse, *Unilever Overseas: the Anatomy of a Multinational, 1895–1965* (London, 1978), pp. 599–600. Sarah Stockwell, *The Business of Decolonization: British Business Strategies in the Gold Coast* (Oxford, 2000). For more on British business and decolonization see Robert L. Tignor, *Capitalism and Nationalism at the End of Empire: State and Business in Decolonizing Egypt, Nigeria and Kenya, 1945–63* (Princeton, 1998); Nicholas White, *Business, Government and the End of Empire: Malaya, 1942–1957* (Oxford, 1996); Nicholas White, 'The Business and the Politics of Decolonization: the British Experience in the Twentieth Century', *Economic History Review*, second series, 53:3 (Aug. 2000), pp. 544–64; and Andrew Cohen, 'Business and Decolonisation in Central Africa Reconsidered', *Journal of Imperial and Commonwealth History*, 36:4 (Dec. 2008), pp. 641–58.

33 Hyam, 'Primacy of Geopolitics', p. 43. See also Ronald Hyam, *Britain's Declining Empire: the Road to Decolonisation, 1918–1968* (Cambridge, 2006).

34 Wm. Roger Louis and Ronald Robinson, 'The Imperialism of Decolonization', *Journal of Imperial and Commonwealth History*, 22:3 (1994), pp. 462–511, quote at p. 473.

35 Howe, *Anticolonialism*, p. 17. For an account of decolonization that emphasizes the role of African nationalism see J. D. Hargreaves, *Decolonization in Africa* (London and New York, 1988).

36 David M. Anderson, 'Mau Mau in the High Court and the "Lost" British Empire Archives: Colonial Conspiracy or Bureaucratic Bungle?', *Journal of Imperial and Commonwealth History*, 39:5 (2011), pp. 699–716, quote at p. 710.

37 Again, work on Kenya has provided the lead here. See David Anderson, *Histories of the Hanged: Britain's Dirty War in Kenya and the End of Empire* (London, 2005) and Caroline Elkins, *Imperial Reckoning: the Untold Story of Britain's Gulag in Kenya* (New York, 2005).

38 P. J. Cain and A. G. Hopkins, *British Imperialism 1688–2000* (London, 2nd Edition, 2001).

39 Schumpeter, 'The Sociology of Imperialisms', pp. 208–14.

40 M. J. Daunton, '"Gentlemanly Capitalism" and British Industry, 1820–1914', *Past & Present*, 122 (Feb. 1989), pp. 119–58. Raymond E. Dumett (ed.), *Gentlemanly Capitalism and British Imperialism: the New Debate on Empire* (Harlow, 1999). Gerold Krozewski, 'Gentlemanly Capitalism and the British Empire after 1945' in Shigeru Akita (ed.), *Gentlemanly Capitalism, Imperialism and Global History* (Basingstoke, 2002), pp. 83–100.

41 Andrew N. Porter, '"Gentlemanly Capitalism" and Empire: the British Experience since 1750?', *Journal of Imperial and Commonwealth History*, 18:2 (Oct. 1990), pp. 265–95. John Darwin, 'Imperialism and the Victorians: the

Dynamics of Territorial Expansion', *English Historical Review*, 112: 447 (Jun. 1997), pp. 614–42.

42 For one recent and fruitful attempt to do this see Andrew Dilley, *Finance, Politics, and Imperialism: Australia, Canada, and the City of London, c.1896–1914* (Basingstoke, 2011).

43 John Gallagher, *The Decline, Revival and Fall of the British Empire: the Ford Lectures and Other Essays* ed. Anil Seal (Cambridge, 1982), p. 75.

44 C. A. Bayly, 'The First Age of Global Imperialism, c.1760–1830', *Journal of Imperial and Commonwealth History*, 26:2 (May 1998), pp. 28–47, quote at p. 28.

45 Ibid., p. 32.

46 C. A. Bayly, *Imperial Meridian: the British Empire and the World, 1780–1830* (London and New York, 1989), pp. 16–74, 105.

47 Ibid., p. 215.

48 Ibid., p. 83.

49 C. A. Bayly, *The Birth of the Modern World, 1780–1914: Global Connections and Comparisons* (Oxford, 2004), pp. 31, 39, 64, 93–95.

50 Ibid., pp. 229, 233.

51 Darwin, 'Imperialism and the Victorians', p. 628.

52 Ibid., p. 617.

53 Ibid., p. 622.

54 Ibid., pp. 626–7.

55 Ibid., p. 636.

56 Ibid., p. 640.

57 Jane Burbank and Frederick Cooper, *Empires in World History: Power and the Politics of Difference* (Princeton, 2010), p. 10.

58 John Darwin, 'Globe and Empire' in Maxine Berg (ed.), *Writing the History of the Global: Challenges for the 21st Century* (Oxford, 2013), pp. 197–9, quote at p. 199.

59 Gallagher and Robinson, 'The Imperialism of Free Trade', p. 9.

60 Osterhammel thus claims that the history of empire can be read as 'a history of the gradual emergence of state structures and societal forms and their geographic expansion or contraction within nominally claimed regions'. Jürgen Osterhammel, *Colonialism: a Theoretical Overview* (Princeton, 1997), p. 28.

61 Fieldhouse, *Economics and Empire*, pp. 476–7.

▶ 2 Control

1 John Darwin, 'Empire and Ethnicity', *Nations and Nationalism*, 16:3, (Jul. 2010), pp. 383–401, quote at p. 384.

2 In his prefatory 'Explanation', in Ronald Robinson and John Gallagher with Alice Denny, *Africa and the Victorians: the Official Mind of Imperialism* (London, 2nd edition, 1981), p. xxi.

3 Ged Martin, 'Canada from 1815' in Andrew Porter (ed.), *The Oxford History of the British Empire* vol. III *The Nineteenth Century* (Oxford, 1999), pp. 522–45, esp. p. 527.

4 Helen Taft Manning, *British Colonial Government after the American Revolution, 1782–1820* (New Haven and London, 1933), pp. 12–13. See also Helen Taft Manning, 'Who Ran the British Empire 1830–1850?', *Journal of British Studies*, 5:1 (Nov., 1965), pp. 88–121.

5 Zoë Laidlaw, *Colonial Connections, 1815–45: Patronage, the Information Revolution and Colonial Government* (Manchester, 2005).

6 Quoted in Darrell Bates, *The Fashoda Incident of 1898: Encounter on the Nile* (Oxford, 1984), p. 72.

7 Christopher Prior, *Exporting Empire: Africa, Colonial Officials and the Construction of the British Imperial State, c. 1900–1939* (Manchester, 2013), p. 172.

8 John Benyon, 'Overlords of Empire? British "Proconsular Imperialism" in Comparative Perspective', *Journal of Imperial and Commonwealth History*, 19:2 (May 1991), pp. 164–202, quotes at pp. 165, 194.

9 Ronald Robinson, 'Non-European Foundations of European Imperialism: Sketch for a Theory of Collaboration' in R. Owen and B. Sutcliffe (eds), *Studies in the Theory of Imperialism* (London, 1972), pp. 117–42, quote at p. 118.

10 Niall Ferguson, *Empire: How Britain Made the Modern World* (London, 2003), pp. 358–9.

11 Eric Stokes, *The English Utilitarians and India* (Oxford, 1959), p. xiii.

12 Joanna Lewis, *Empire State-Building: War and Welfare in Kenya, 1925–52* (Oxford, 2000), p. 373.

13 Jürgen Osterhammel, *Colonialism: a Theoretical Overview* (Princeton, 1997), p. 57.

14 Bernard Cohn, *Colonialism and its Forms of Knowledge: the British in India* (Princeton, 1996), pp. 3–4, quote at p. 4.

15 Jon E. Wilson, *The Domination of Strangers: Modern Governance in Eastern India, 1780–1835* (Basingstoke, 2008).

16 Miles Taylor, 'Imperium et Libertas? Rethinking the Radical Critique of Imperialism during the Nineteenth Century', *Journal of Imperial and Commonwealth History*, 19:1 (Jan. 1991), pp. 1–23.

17 J. A. Hobson, *Imperialism: a Study* (London, 3rd Edition, 1988 [1938]), pp. 223–84.

18 John L. Comaroff, 'Reflections on the Colonial State, in South Africa and Elsewhere: Factions, Fragments, Facts and Fictions', *Social Identities*, 4:3 (1998), pp. 321–61, quote at p. 336.

19 John Darwin, *Unfinished Empire: the Global Expansion of Britain* (London, 2012), pp. 194–202.

20 James Belich, *Replenishing the Earth: the Settler Revolution and the Rise of the Anglo-World, 1783–1939* (Oxford, 2009), pp. 185–92.

21 Donald Denoon, *Settler Capitalism: the Dynamics of Dependent Development in the Southern Hemisphere* (Oxford, 1983).

22 Robinson and Gallagher, *Africa and the Victorians*, p. 56.

23 A. F. Madden, '"Not for Export": the Westminster Model of Government and British Colonial Practice' in N. Hillmer and P. Wigley (eds), *The First British Commonwealth: Essays in Honour of Nicholas Mansergh* (London, 1980), pp. 10–29.

24 Darwin, *Unfinished Empire*, pp. 202–22.

25 Lewis, *Empire State-Building*, pp. 2, 7.

26 Comaroff, 'Reflections on the Colonial State', p. 335.

27 Jonathan Saha, *Law, Disorder and the Colonial State: Corruption in Burma, c. 1900* (Basingstoke, 2013), p. 2. See also D. A. Washbrook, *The Emergence of Provincial Politics: the Madras Presidency, 1870–1920* (Cambridge, 1976), pp. 45–7.

28 Shula Marks and Stanley Trapido, 'Lord Milner and the South African State', *History Workshop*, 8 (Autumn 1979), pp. 50–80, quote at p. 52.

29 A. N. Porter, *The Origins of the South African War: Joseph Chamberlain and the Diplomacy of Imperialism, 1895–99* (Manchester, 1980). Iain R. Smith, *The Origins of the South African War, 1899–1902* (London and New York, 1996).

30 Comaroff, 'Reflections on the Colonial State', pp. 327–8, 337.

31 Ann Laura Stoler and Frederick Cooper, 'Between Metropole and Colony: Rethinking a Research Agenda' in Frederick Cooper and Ann Laura Stoler (eds), *Tensions of Empire: Colonial Cultures in a Bourgeois World* (Berkeley, Los Angeles, and London, 1997), p. 19. For more on this see Bruce Berman and John Lonsdale, *Unhappy Valley: Conflict in Kenya & Africa* (London, 2 vols, 1992).

32 D. K. Fieldhouse, *Merchant Capital and Economic Decolonization: the United Africa Company, 1929–1987* (Oxford, 1994), p. 82.

33 David Washbrook, 'The Indian Economy and the British Empire' in Douglas M. Peers and Nandini Gooptu (eds), *India and the British Empire* (Oxford, 2012), pp. 44–74, quote at p. 51.

34 Douglas M. Peers, 'State, Power, and Colonialism' in Peers and Gooptu (eds), *India and the British Empire*, pp. 16–43, esp. p. 19.

35 Ibid., p. 17.

36 Washbrook, 'The Indian Economy and the British Empire', p. 72.

37 C. A. Bayly, *The Birth of the Modern World, 1780–1914: Global Connections and Comparisons* (Oxford, 2004), p. 254.

38 Anil Seal, *The Emergence of Indian Nationalism: Competition and Collaboration in the Later Nineteenth Century* (Cambridge, 1968), pp. 8–9.

39 Ibid., p. 12.

40 D. A. Washbrook, *The Emergence of Provincial Politics: the Madras Presidency, 1870–1920* (Cambridge, 1976), quote at p. 45. See also Gordon Johnson, *Provincial Politics and Indian Nationalism: Bombay and the Indian National Congress 1880 to 1915* (Cambridge, 1973), esp. pp. 6–7, and the essays in John Gallagher, Gordon Johnson, and Anil Seal (eds), *Locality, Province and Nation: Essays on Indian Politics 1870 to 1940* (Cambridge, 1973), also available as a special issue of *Modern Asian Studies*, 7:3 (Jul. 1973).

41 Ronald Robinson, 'The Excentric Idea of Imperialism, With or Without Empire', in Wolfgang J. Mommsen and Jürgen Osterhammel (eds), *Imperialism and After: Continuities and Discontinuities* (London, 1986), pp. 267–89.

42 Robinson, 'Non-European Foundations of European Imperialism', p. 118.

43 Colin Newbury, *Patrons, Clients, and Empire: Chieftaincy and Over-Rule in Asia, Africa, and the Pacific* (Oxford, 2003).

44 Tony Ballantyne, 'Colonial Knowledge', in Sarah Stockwell (ed.), *The British Empire: Themes and Perspectives* (Malden and Oxford, 2008), pp. 177–97, quotes at p. 177.

45 Nicholas B. Dirks, *Castes of Mind: Colonialism and the Making of Modern India* (Princeton, 2001), p. ix.

46 Michel Foucault, 'Governmentality' in Graham Burchell, Colin Gordon, and Peter Miller (eds) *The Foucault Effect: Studies in Governmentality* (Chicago, 1991), pp. 87–104. Deana Heath, *Purifying Empire: Obscenity and the Politics of Moral Regulation in Britain, India and Australia* (Cambridge, 2010), p. 8.

47 Edward Said, *Orientalism* (New York, 1978).

48 Ballantyne, 'Colonial Knowledge', p. 178.

49 Dirks, *Castes of Mind*, p. 9.

50 Cohn, *Colonialism and its Forms of Knowledge*, pp. 5–11, quotes at pp. 16, 21.

51 Dirks, *Castes of Mind*, quote at p. 9, emphasis added.

52 C. A. Bayly, *Empire and Information: Intelligence Gathering and Social Communication in India, 1780–1870* (Cambridge, 1996), p. 314.

53 Norbert Peabody, 'Knowledge Formation in Colonial India' in Peers and Gooptu (eds), *India and the British Empire*, pp. 75–99, esp. p. 77. Tony Ballantyne, *Orientalism and Race: Aryanism in the British Empire* (Basingstoke, 2002), p. 194.

54 Bayly, *Empire and Information*. C. A. Bayly, 'Knowing the Country: Empire and Information in India', *Modern Asian Studies*, 27:1 (Feb. 1993), pp. 3–43.

55 Frederick Cooper, *Colonialism in Question: Theory, Knowledge, History* (Berkeley, 2005), p. 143.

56 Prior, *Exporting Empire*, p. 10.

57 Ibid., p. 97.

58 Ulrike von Hirschhausen and Jörn Leonhard, 'Beyond Rise, Decline and Fall: Comparing Multi-Ethnic Empires in the Long Nineteenth Century' in Jörn Leonhard and Ulrike von Hirschhausen (eds), *Comparing Empires: Encounters and Transfers in the Long Nineteenth Century* (Göttingen, 2011), pp. 9–34, quote at p. 16.

59 Osterhammel, *Colonialism*, p. 58.

60 For more on famine and empire see Mike Davis, *Late Victorian Holocausts: El Niño Famines and the Making of the Third World* (London, 2001).

61 Lewis, *Empire State-Building*, p. 374.

▶ 3 Difference

1 Ronald Hyam, *Britain's Declining Empire: the Road to Decolonisation, 1918–1968* (Cambridge, 2006), p. 1.

2 A. N. Porter, *Religion versus Empire? British Protestant Missionaries and Overseas Expansion, 1700–1914* (Manchester, 2004).

3 John L. Comaroff, 'Reflections on the Colonial State, in South Africa and Elsewhere: Factions, Fragments, Facts and Fictions', *Social Identities*, 4:3 (1998), pp. 321–61, p. 329.

4 Partha Chatterjee, *The Nation and its Fragments* (Princeton, 1993), p. 10.

5 Jane Burbank and Frederick Cooper, *Empires in World History: Power and the Politics of Difference* (Princeton, 2010), p. 8.

6 Timothy Mitchell, *Colonising Egypt* (Cambridge, 1988), p. 167.

7 Susan Bayly, 'The Evolution of Colonial Cultures: Nineteenth-Century Asia' in Andrew Porter (ed.), *The Oxford History of the British Empire* vol. III *The Nineteenth Century* (Oxford, 1999), pp. 447–69, quote at p. 447.

8 D. A. Washbrook, 'Progress and Problems: South Asian Economic and Social History c.1720–1860', *Modern Asian Studies*, 22:1 (Feb. 1988), pp. 57–96, quote at p. 85.

9 Nicholas B. Dirks, *Castes of Mind: Colonialism and the Making of Modern India* (Princeton, 2001), quotes at pp. 5, 10.

10 Ibid., p. 313.

11 Chatterjee, *The Nation and its Fragments*, pp. 31–2.

12 C. A. Bayly, *Empire and Information: Intelligence Gathering and Social Communication in India, 1780-1870* (Cambridge, 1996), p. 142.

13 Susan Bayly, *Caste, Society and Politics in India from the Eighteenth Century to the Modern Age* (Cambridge, 1999).

14 John Darwin, 'Empire and Ethnicity', *Nations and Nationalism*, 16:3 (Jul. 2010), pp. 383–401, quote at p. 386.

15 E. P. Thompson, *The Making of the English Working Class* (London, 1963).

16 Raymond Williams, *Marxism and Literature* (Oxford, 1977), p. 110.

17 Ranajit Guha, 'On some Aspects of the Historiography of Colonial India', *Subaltern Studies I: Writings on South Asian History and Society* (Delhi, 1982), p. 2.

18 Chatterjee, *The Nation and its Fragments*, p. 167. For a critique of this approach see Jon E. Wilson, '"A Thousand Countries to Go to": Peasants and Rulers in Late Eighteenth-Century Bengal', *Past & Present*, 189 (Nov., 2005), pp. 81–109.

19 Jon E. Wilson, 'Subjects and Agents in the History of Imperialism and Resistance' in David Scott and Charles Hirschkind (eds), *Powers of the Secular Modern: Talal Asad and his Interlocutors* (Stanford, 2006), pp. 180–205, quote at p. 181.

20 Terence Ranger, 'The Invention of Tradition in Tropical Africa' in Eric Hobsbawm and Terence Ranger (eds), *The Invention of Tradition* (Cambridge, 1983), pp. 211–262, quote at p. 212.

21 Christine Bolt, *Victorian Attitudes to Race* (London, 1971).

22 Compare Nancy Stepan, *The Idea of Race in Science: Great Britain, 1800–1960* (London and Basingstoke, 1982) with Douglas Lorimer, *Science, Race Relations and Resistance: Britain, 1870–1914* (Manchester, 2013).

23 C. A. Bayly 'The First Age of Global Imperialism, c.1760–1830', *Journal of Imperial and Commonwealth History*, 26:2 (May 1998), pp. 28–47, quote p. 39.

24 David Cannadine, *Ornamentalism: How the British Saw Their Empire* (London, 2001). For various critiques of Cannadine's book see Tony Ballantyne (ed.), *From Orientalism to Ornamentalism: Empire and Difference in History*, a special issue of the *Journal of Colonialism and Colonial History*, 3:1 (April 2002).

25 C. A. Bayly, *The Birth of the Modern World, 1780–1914: Global Connections and Comparisons* (Oxford, 2004), p. 221.

26 Sean Hawkins and Philip D. Morgan, 'Blacks and the British Empire: an Introduction' in Philip D. Morgan and Sean Hawkins (eds), *Black Experience and the Empire* (Oxford, 2004), pp. 1–34. Laura Tabili, *'We Ask for British Justice': Workers and Racial Difference in Late Imperial Britain* (Ithaca, 1994).

27 Alan Lester, 'British Settler Discourse and the Circuits of Empire', *History Workshop Journal*, 54 (Autumn 2002), pp. 24–48, esp. p. 40.

28 Bolt, *Victorian Attitudes to Race*. Catherine Hall, *Civilising Subjects: Metropole and Colony in the English Imagination, 1830–1867* (Oxford, 2002).

29 Douglas A. Lorimer, *Colour, Class and the Victorians: English Attitudes to the Negro in the Mid-Nineteenth Century* (Leicester, 1978), p. 189.

30 T. C. McCaskie, 'Cultural Encounters: Britain and Africa in the Nineteenth Century' in Morgan and Hawkins (eds), *Black Experience and the Empire*, pp. 166–93.

31 Damon Ieremia Salesa, *Racial Crossings: Race, Intermarriage, and the Victorian British Empire* (Oxford, 2011), quote at p. 2.

32 Lorimer, *Science, Race Relations and Resistance*, p. 24.
33 Vivian Bickford-Smith, 'The Betrayal of Creole Elites, 1880–1920' in Morgan and Hawkins (eds), *Black Experience and the Empire*, pp. 194–227.
34 Hawkins and Morgan, 'Blacks and the British Empire', p. 17.
35 Angela Woollacott, *Gender and Empire* (Basingstoke, 2006), pp. 1, 3.
36 Kathleen Wilson, 'Empire, Gender, and Modernity in the Eighteenth Century' in Philippa Levine (ed.), *Gender and Empire* (Oxford, 2004), pp. 14–45. esp. pp. 28–34.
37 Anne McClintock, *Imperial Leather: Race, Gender and Sexuality in the Colonial Contest* (New York and London, 1995), p. 7.
38 Clare Midgley, *Women against Slavery: the British Campaigns, 1780–1870* (London, 1992), quote at p. 200.
39 Antoinette Burton, *Burdens of History: British Feminists, Indian Women and Imperial Culture, 1865–1915* (Chapel Hill, North Carolina, 1994).
40 Lisa Chilton, *Agents of Empire: British Female Migration to Canada and Australia, 1860s–1930* (Toronto, 2007). See also Katie Pickles, *Female Imperialism and National Identity: Imperial Order Daughters of the Empire* (Manchester, 2009).
41 Joanna Lewis, *Empire State-Building: War and Welfare in Kenya, 1925–52* (Oxford, 2000), pp. 11–12.
42 Philippa Levine, *Prostitution, Race and Politics: Policing Venereal Disease in the British Empire* (New York and London, 2003).
43 Catherine Hall, 'Of Gender and Empire: Reflections on the Nineteenth Century' in Levine (ed.), *Gender and Empire*, pp. 46–76, esp. p. 52.
44 Diana Jeater, 'The British Empire and African Women in the Twentieth Century' in Morgan and Hawkins (eds), *Black Experience and the Empire*, pp. 228–56, quote at p. 241.
45 Philippa Levine, 'Sexuality, Gender, and Empire', in Levine (ed.), *Gender and Empire*, pp. 134–55, quote at pp. 139–40.
46 Robert Aldrich, *Colonialism and Homosexuality* (London and New York, 2003), p. 4.
47 Mrinalini Sinha, *Colonial Masculinity, the 'Manly Englishman' and the 'Effeminate Bengali' in the Late Nineteenth Century* (Manchester, 1995), p. 7.
48 Lorimer, *Science, Race Relations and Resistance*, p. 192.
49 Heather Streets, *Martial Races: the Military, Race and Masculinity in British Imperial Culture, 1857–1914* (Manchester, 2004), quote at p. 7.
50 Philippa Levine, 'Preface' in Levine (ed.), *Gender and Empire*, pp. vii–x, quote at p. ix.
51 Joanna de Groot, '"Sex" and "Race": the Construction of Language and Image in the Nineteenth Century' in Catherine Hall (ed.), *Cultures of Empire: Colonizers in Britain and the Empire in the Nineteenth and Twentieth Centuries – a Reader* (Manchester, 2000), pp. 37–60, quote at p. 38.

52 Ann Laura Stoler, *Race and the Education of Desire: Foucault's* History of Sexuality *and the Colonial Order of Things* (Durham, 1995).

53 Antoinette Burton, 'Rules of Thumb: British History and "Imperial Culture" in Nineteenth and Twentieth-Century Britain', *Women's History Review*, 3:4 (Dec. 1994), pp. 483–501.

54 Andrew Porter, '"Cultural Imperialism" and Protestant Missionary Enterprise, 1780–1914', *Journal of Imperial and Commonwealth History*, 25:3 (Sept. 1997), pp. 367–91, quote at p. 373.

55 Ibid., pp. 373–4.

► 4 Identity

1 Jane Burbank and Frederick Cooper, *Empires in World History: Power and the Politics of Difference* (Princeton, 2010), p. 13.

2 Partha Chatterjee, *The Nation and its Fragments* (Princeton, 1993), p. 10.

3 Ronald Hyam, *Britain's Declining Empire: the Road to Decolonisation, 1918–1968* (Cambridge, 2006), pp. 257–61.

4 Ronald Robinson and John Gallagher with Alice Denny, *Africa and the Victorians: the Official Mind of Imperialism* (London, 2nd edition, 1981), quotes at pp. 465, 469, 470.

5 Ronald Robinson, 'Non-European Foundations of European Imperialism: Sketch for a Theory of Collaboration' in R. Owen and B. Sutcliffe (eds), *Studies in the Theory of Imperialism* (London, 1972), pp. 117–42, quote at p. 139.

6 Benedict Anderson, *Imagined Communities: Reflections on the Origin and Spread of Nationalism* (London, 1983). Ernest Gellner, *Nations and Nationalism* (Oxford, 1983). Eric Hobsbawm, *Nations and Nationalism since 1780: Programme, Myth, Reality* (Cambridge, 1990).

7 C. A. Bayly, *The Birth of the Modern World, 1780–1914: Global Connections and Comparisons* (Oxford, 2004), pp. 227–8.

8 Anil Seal, *The Emergence of Indian Nationalism: Competition and Collaboration in the Later Nineteenth Century* (Cambridge, 1968).

9 Anil Seal, 'Imperialism and Nationalism in India' in John Gallagher, Gordon Johnson, and Anil Seal (eds), *Locality, Province and Nation: Essays on Indian Politics 1870 to 1940* (Cambridge, 1973), pp. 1–28, quote at p. 27. See also Gordon Johnson, *Provincial Politics and Indian Nationalism: Bombay and the Indian National Congress 1880 to 1915* (Cambridge, 1973) and D. A. Washbrook, *The Emergence of Provincial Politics: the Madras Presidency, 1870–1920* (Cambridge, 1976).

10 Seal, *The Emergence of Indian Nationalism*, p. 351.

11 Chatterjee, *The Nation and its Fragments*, pp. 6, 10.

12 Jürgen Osterhammel, *Colonialism: a Theoretical Overview* (Princeton, 1997), p. 95.

13 John Darwin, *Unfinished Empire: the Global Expansion of Britain* (London, 2012), pp. 301–2.

14 For a detailed discussion of theories of cultural imperialism see John Tomlinson, *Cultural Imperialism: a Critical Introduction* (Baltimore, 1991).

15 Su Lin Lewis, 'Echoes of Cosmopolitanism: Colonial Penang's "Indigenous" English Press' in Chandrika Kaul (ed.), *Media and the British Empire* (Basingstoke, 2006), pp. 233–49, quote at p. 246.

16 Susan Bayly, 'The Evolution of Colonial Cultures: Nineteenth-Century Asia' in Andrew Porter (ed.), *The Oxford History of the British Empire* vol. III *The Nineteenth Century* (Oxford, 1999), pp. 447–69, quotes at pp. 459, 466.

17 Howard Johnson, 'The Black Experience in the British Caribbean in the Twentieth Century' in Philip D. Morgan and Sean Hawkins (eds), *Black Experience and the Empire* (Oxford, 2004), pp. 317–46, quote at p. 339. For the classic work on cricket see C. L. R. James, *Beyond a Boundary* (Durham, 2013 [1963]).

18 Anne Spry Rush, 'Imperial Identity in Colonial Minds: Harold Moody and the League of Coloured Peoples, 1931–50', *Twentieth Century British History*, 13:4 (2002), pp. 356–83, quote at p. 360.

19 Sean Hawkins and Philip D. Morgan, 'Blacks and the British Empire: an Introduction' in Morgan and Hawkins (eds), *Black Experience and the Empire*, pp. 1–34, esp. p. 3.

20 Vivian Bickford-Smith, 'The Betrayal of Creole Elites, 1880–1920' in Morgan and Hawkins (eds), *Black Experience and the Empire*, pp. 194–227.

21 Bill Nasson, 'Black Communities in Natal and the Cape' in David Omissi and Andrew Thompson (eds), *The Impact of the South African War* (Basingstoke, 2002), pp. 38–55. Christopher Saunders, 'African Attitudes to Britain and the Empire Before and After the South African War' in Donal Lowry (ed.), *The South African War Reappraised* (Manchester, 2000), pp. 140–9. Hilary Sapire, 'African Loyalism and its Discontents: the Royal Tour of South Africa, 1947', *Historical Journal*, 54:1 (Mar. 2011), pp. 215–40.

22 John Gallagher, *The Decline, Revival and Fall of the British Empire: the Ford Lectures and Other Essays* ed. Anil Seal (Cambridge, 1982), p. 148.

23 John Darwin, *After Tamerlane: the Global History of Empire since 1405* (London, 2007), p. 347.

24 Anderson, *Imagined Communities*, ch. 6.

25 Jan Nederveen Pieterse, *Empire and Emancipation: Power and Liberation on a World Scale* (London, 1990), pp. 181–5.

26 Freda Harcourt, 'Disraeli's Imperialism, 1866–1868: a Question of Timing', *Historical Journal*, 23:1 (Mar. 1980), pp. 87–109.

27 Stephen Howe, 'Empire and Ideology' in Sarah Stockwell (ed.), *The British Empire: Themes and Perspectives* (Malden and Oxford, 2008), pp. 157–76, esp. p. 172. John M. MacKenzie, 'Introduction' in John M. MacKenzie (ed.), *European Empires and the People: Popular Responses to Imperialism in France, Britain, the Netherlands, Belgium, Germany and Italy* (Manchester and New York, 2011), pp. 1–18, esp. pp. 4–5.

28 A. N. Porter, *The Origins of the South African War: Joseph Chamberlain and the Diplomacy of Imperialism, 1895–99* (Manchester, 1980).

29 Penny Summerfield, 'Patriotism and Empire: Music Hall Entertainment, 1870–1914' in John M. MacKenzie (ed.), *Imperialism and Popular Culture* (Manchester, 1986), pp. 17–48, quote at p. 25.

30 J. A. Hobson, *The Psychology of Jingoism* (London, 1901), p. 1.

31 Ibid., pp. 6–8.

32 Ibid., pp. 9–10.

33 J. A. Hobson, *The War in South Africa: its Causes and Effects* (London, 1900), pp. 206–7, quote at p. 215.

34 Simon J. Potter, *News and the British World: the Emergence of an Imperial Press System, 1876–1922* (Oxford, 2003), pp. 36–55.

35 MacKenzie, 'Introduction', pp. 1–2.

36 John M. MacKenzie, *Propaganda and Empire* (Manchester, 1984), quotes at pp. 2, 253–4.

37 John M. MacKenzie, 'The Press and the Dominant Ideology of Empire' in Simon J. Potter (ed.), *Newspapers and Empire in Ireland and Britain: Reporting the British Empire, c. 1857–1921* (Dublin, 2004), pp. 23–38. Stephen Heathorn, *For Home, Country, and Race: Constructing Gender, Class, and Englishness in the Elementary School, 1880–1914* (Toronto, 2000), p. 211.

38 Ann Laura Stoler and Frederick Cooper, 'Between Metropole and Colony: Rethinking a Research Agenda' in Frederick Cooper and Ann Laura Stoler (eds), *Tensions of Empire: Colonial Cultures in a Bourgeois World* (Berkeley and London, 1997), p. 15.

39 Linda Colley, 'Britishness and Otherness: an Argument', *Journal of British Studies*, 31:4 (Oct. 1992), pp. 309–29, quotes at pp. 312, 316, 325. See also Linda Colley, *Britons: Forging the Nation, 1707–1837* (New Haven, 1992).

40 Kathleen Wilson, 'Introduction: Histories, Empires, Modernities', in Kathleen Wilson (ed.), *A New Imperial History: Culture, Identity and Modernity in Britain and the Empire, 1660–1840* (Cambridge, 2004), pp. 1–26, esp. pp. 3–4.

41 Antoinette Burton, 'Introduction: on the Inadequacy and the Indispensability of the Nation' in Antoinette Burton (ed.), *After the Imperial Turn: Thinking With and Through the Nation* (Durham, 2003), pp. 1–23, quote at p. 3.

42 Edward W. Said, *Orientalism* (New York, 1978). See also Said's *Culture and Imperialism* (New York, 1993). For a critical discussion of Said and post-colonial theory see David Washbrook, 'Orients and Occidents: Colonial Discourse Theory and the Historiography of the British Empire' in Robin Winks (ed.), *The Oxford History of the British Empire* vol. V *Historiography* (Oxford, 1999), pp. 596–611.

43 Catherine Hall, 'The Rule of Difference: Gender, Class and Empire in the Making of the 1832 Reform Act' in Ida Blom, Karen Hagemann, and Catherine Hall (eds), *Gendered Nations: Nationalism and Gender Order in the Long Nineteenth Century* (Oxford, 2000), pp. 107–35, quotes at pp. 108, 112.

44 Catherine Hall, 'The Nation Within and Without' in Catherine Hall, Keith McClelland, and Jane Rendall (eds), *Defining the Victorian Nation: Class, Race, Gender and the Reform Act of 1867* (Cambridge, 2000), pp. 179–233.

45 Catherine Hall, *Civilising Subjects: Metropole and Colony in the English Imagination, 1830–1867* (Oxford, 2002), quotes at pp. 8, 12.

46 Catherine Hall and Sonya Rose, 'Introduction: Being at Home with the Empire' in Catherine Hall and Sonya O. Rose (eds), *At Home with the Empire: Metropolitan Culture and the Imperial World* (Cambridge, 2006), pp. 1–31, quotes at pp. 22–3.

47 Bernard Porter, *The Absent-Minded Imperialists: Empire, Society, and Culture in Britain* (Oxford, 2004), p. 115.

48 Peter Mandler, '"Race" and "Nation" in Mid-Victorian Thought' in Stefan Collini, Richard Whatmore, and Brian Young (eds), *History, Religion, and Culture: British Intellectual History, 1750–1950* (Cambridge, 2000), pp. 224–44.

49 For a more detailed discussion see Simon J. Potter, 'Empire, Cultures and Identities in Nineteenth- and Twentieth-Century Britain', *History Compass*, 5:1 (Jan. 2007), pp. 51–71.

50 P. J. Marshall, 'Imperial Britain', *Journal of Imperial and Commonwealth History*, 23:3 (Sept. 1995), pp. 379–94.

51 Andrew S. Thompson, *The Empire Strikes Back? The Impact of Imperialism on Britain from the Mid-Nineteenth Century* (Harlow, 2005).

52 John M. MacKenzie, 'Empire and National Identities: the Case of Scotland', *Transactions of the Royal Historical Society*, sixth series, 8 (1998), pp. 215–31.

53 Potter (ed.), *Newspapers and Empire*.

54 Darwin, *Unfinished Empire*, pp. 292–3.

55 Carl Bridge and Kent Fedorowich, 'Mapping the British World', *Journal of Imperial and Commonwealth History*, 31:2 (May 2003), pp. 1–15. Also available in Carl Bridge and Kent Fedorowich (eds), *The British World: Diaspora, Culture, Identity* (London, 2003), pp. 1–15.

56 For a fuller discussion of this issue, focusing on the case of Canada, see Phillip Buckner and R. Douglas Francis, 'Introduction', in Phillip Buckner and R. Douglas Francis (eds), *Canada and the British World: Culture, Migration, and Identity* (Vancouver, 2005), pp. 1–9.

57 Richard Jebb, *Studies in Colonial Nationalism* (London, 1905), pp. 84, 99–100.

58 On the Canadian case see Ged Martin, *Britain and the Origins of Canadian Confederation, 1837–67* (Vancouver, 1995). On the enduring idea of federalism as a tool of British imperial interests see Martin Kolinsky, 'Federation and Partition in the Transformation of Empire' in C. Navari (ed.), *British Politics and the Spirit of the Age: Political Concepts in Action* (Keele, 1996), pp. 159–73.

59 For more on Jebb see J. D. B Miller, *Richard Jebb and the Problem of Empire* (London, 1956) and Simon J. Potter, 'Richard Jebb, John S. Ewart, and the Round Table, 1898–1926', *English Historical Review*, 122: 495 (Feb. 2007), pp. 105–32.

60 See for example Norman Penlington, *Canada and Imperialism, 1896–1899* (Toronto, 1965) and Carl Berger, *The Sense of Power: Studies in the Ideas of Canadian Imperialism, 1867–1914* (Toronto, 1970).

61 Douglas L. Cole, 'The Problem of "Nationalism" and "Imperialism" in British Settlement Colonies', *Journal of British Studies*, 10:2 (May 1971), pp. 160–82.

62 Neville Meaney, 'Britishness and Australian Identity: the Problem of Nationalism in Australian History and Historiography', *Australian Historical Studies*, 32:116 (Apr. 2001), pp. 76–90; Stuart Ward, *Australia and the British Embrace: the Demise of the Imperial Ideal* (Carlton, Vic., 2001), pp. 1–12.

63 James Curran and Stuart Ward, *The Unknown Nation: Australia after Empire* (Carlton, Vic., 2010), p. 7.

64 See, most famously, George Grant, *Lament for a Nation: the Defeat of Canadian Nationalism* (Princeton, 1965).

65 Bridge and Fedorowich, 'Mapping the British World', p. 4.

66 James Belich, *Replenishing the Earth: the Settler Revolution and the Rise of the Anglo-World, 1783–1939* (Oxford, 2009).

67 Ged Martin, 'Canada from 1815' in Andrew Porter (ed.), *The Oxford History of the British Empire* vol. III *The Nineteenth Century* (Oxford, 1999), pp. 522–45, esp. p. 535.

68 Gary B. Magee and Andrew S. Thompson, *Empire and Globalisation: Networks of People, Goods and Capital in the British World, c.1850–1914* (Cambridge, 2010), p. 118.

69 Kent Fedorowich and Andrew S. Thompson (eds), *Empire, Migration and Identity in the British World* (Manchester, 2013).

70 Helen Taft Manning, 'Who Ran the British Empire 1830–1850?', *Journal of British Studies*, 5:1 (Nov. 1965), pp. 88–121, esp. p. 93.
71 Bridge and Fedorowich, 'Mapping the British World', p. 3.
72 Phillip Buckner and R. Douglas Francis, 'Introduction', in Phillip Buckner and R. Douglas Francis (eds), *Rediscovering the British World* (Calgary, 2005), pp. 9–20, esp. p. 15.
73 Simon J. Potter, *Broadcasting Empire: the BBC and the British World, 1922–1970* (Oxford, 2012).
74 Tamson Pietsch, *Empire of Scholars: Universities, Networks and the British Academic World, 1850–1939* (Manchester, 2013), quote at p. 61.
75 Alan Lester, 'Imperial Circuits and Networks: Geographies of the British Empire', *History Compass*, 4:1 (Jan. 2006), pp. 124–41, quote at p. 130.
76 R. Scott Sheffield, 'Rehabilitating the Indigene: Post-War Reconstruction and the Image of the Indigenous Other in English Canada and New Zealand, 1943–1948' in Buckner and Francis (eds), *Rediscovering the British World*, pp, 341–60.
77 Rachel Bright, 'Asian Migration and the British World, c. 1850–c. 1914' in Fedorowich and Thompson (eds), *Empire, Migration and Identity in the British World*, pp. 128–49, quote at p. 128.
78 Donal Lowry, 'The Crown, Empire Loyalism and the Assimilation of Non-British White Subjects in the British World: an Argument against "Ethnic Determinism"', *Journal of Imperial and Commonwealth History*, 31:2 (May 2003), pp. 96–120. Also available in Bridge and Fedorowich (eds), *The British World*, pp. 96–120.

▶ 5 Going Global

1 John L. Comaroff, 'Reflections on the Colonial State, in South Africa and Elsewhere: Factions, Fragments, Facts and Fictions', *Social Identities*, 4:3 (1998), pp. 321–61, quote at p. 321.
2 Wolfgang J. Mommsen, *Theories of Imperialism* (London, 1980), p. 31.
3 Andre Gunder Frank, *Capitalism and Underdevelopment in Latin America: Historical Studies of Chile and Brazil* (New York, 1967). Immanuel Wallerstein, *The Modern World System* (New York, 4 vols, 1974–2011).
4 Kenneth Pomeranz, *The Great Divergence: China, Europe, and the Making of the Modern World Economy* (Princeton, 2000), quote at p. 4.
5 See also Kevin Grant, Philippa Levine, and Frank Trentmann (eds), *Beyond Sovereignty: Britain, Empire and Transnationalism 1860–1950* (Basingstoke, 2007).
6 Simon J. Potter, *News and the British World: the Emergence of an Imperial Press System, 1876–1922* (Oxford, 2003).

7 Richard H. Grove, *Green Imperialism: Colonial Expansion, Tropical Island Edens and the Origins of Environmentalism, 1600–1860* (Cambridge, 1995). Richard Drayton, *Nature's Government: Science, Imperial Britain, and the 'Improvement' of the World* (New Haven, 2000). Alfred W. Crosby, *Ecological Imperialism: the Biological Expansion of Europe, 900–1900* (Cambridge, 1986).

8 John Darwin, *After Tamerlane: the Global History of Empire since 1405* (London, 2007), p. 12.

9 Tom Friedman, *The Lexus and the Olive Tree: Understanding Globalization* (New York, 2000), p. xvi.

10 David Fieldhouse, 'Can Humpty-Dumpty Be Put Together Again? Imperial History in the 1980s', *Journal of Imperial and Commonwealth History*, 12:2 (Jan. 1984), pp. 9–23.

11 A. G. Hopkins, 'Back to the Future: from National History to Imperial History, *Past & Present*, 164 (Aug., 1999), pp. 198–243.

12 For further discussion of these two opposing positions see John Darwin, 'Globalism and Imperialism: the Global Context of British Power, 1830–1960' in Shigeru Akita (ed.), *Gentlemanly Capitalism, Imperialism and Global History* (Basingstoke, 2002), pp. 43–64.

13 Jan Nederveen Pieterse, *Globalization or Empire?* (New York and London, 2004), quote at p. v.

14 Herbert Lüthy, 'Colonization and the Making of Mankind', *Journal of Economic History*, 21: 4 (Dec. 1961), pp. 483–95, quotes at pp. 485, 486, 488, 495.

15 Ibid., quotes at pp. 490, 494, 495.

16 Niall Ferguson, *Empire: How Britain Made the Modern World* (London, 2003).

17 D. A. Washbrook, 'Progress and Problems: South Asian Economic and Social History c.1720–1860', *Modern Asian Studies*, 22:1 (Feb. 1988), pp. 57–96.

18 Darwin, *After Tamerlane*, p. 23. On this point see also Jane Burbank and Frederick Cooper, *Empires in World History: Power and the Politics of Difference* (Princeton, 2010), pp. 2–3.

19 Darwin, *After Tamerlane*, p. 60.

20 Ibid., pp. 6, 16.

21 Ibid., pp. 6, 409, 482.

22 C. A. Bayly, *The Birth of the Modern World, 1780–1914: Global Connections and Comparisons* (Oxford, 2004). See also Andre Gunder Frank, *ReORIENT: Global Economy in the Asian Age* (Berkeley and Los Angeles, 1998).

23 Bernhard Struck, Kate Ferris, and Jacques Revel, "Introduction: Space and Scale in Transnational History," *International History Review*, 33:4 (Dec. 2011), pp. 573–84 quote at pp. 573–4.

24 Pierre-Yves Saunier, *Transnational History* (Basingstoke, 2013), p. 57.

25 See, most notably, Manuel Castells, *The Rise of the Network Society* (Oxford, 1996).

26 Tony Ballantyne, *Orientalism and Race: Aryanism in the British Empire* (Basingstoke, 2002), quote at p. 195.

27 Alan Lester, *Imperial Networks: Creating Identities in Nineteenth-Century South Africa and Britain* (London and New York, 2001), pp. 6–8. Alan Lester, 'British Settler Discourse and the Circuits of Empire', *History Workshop Journal*, 54 (Autumn 2002), pp. 24–48.

28 Alan Lester, 'Imperial Circuits and Networks: Geographies of the British Empire', *History Compass*, 4:1 (Jan. 2006), pp. 124–41, quote at p. 124.

29 Ronald Robinson, 'The Excentric Idea of Imperialism, With or Without Empire', in Wolfgang J. Mommsen and Jürgen Osterhammel (eds), *Imperialism and After: Continuities and Discontinuities* (London, 1986), pp. 267–89, quote at p. 270.

30 Kent Fedorowich and Andrew S. Thompson, 'Mapping the Contours of the British World: Empire, Migration and Identity' in Kent Fedorowich and Andrew S. Thompson (eds), *Empire, Migration and Identity in the British World* (Manchester, 2013), pp. 1–41, quote at p. 2.

31 Gary B. Magee and Andrew S. Thompson, *Empire and Globalisation: Networks of People, Goods and Capital in the British World, c.1850–1914* (Cambridge, 2010), p. xiii.

32 Tamson Pietsch, 'Rethinking the British World', *Journal of British Studies*, 52:2 (Apr. 2013), pp. 441–63.

33 Bayly, *Birth of the Modern World*, p. 476.

34 Zoë Laidlaw, *Colonial Connections, 1815–45: Patronage, the Information Revolution and Colonial Government* (Manchester, 2005).

35 Simon J. Potter, *Broadcasting Empire: the BBC and the British World, 1922–1970* (Oxford, 2012).

36 Frederick Cooper, *Colonialism in Question: Theory, Knowledge, History* (Berkeley and Los Angeles, 2005), p. 91.

37 B. R. Tomlinson, 'Economics and Empire: the Periphery and the Imperial Economy' in Andrew Porter (ed.), *The Oxford History of the British Empire* vol. III *The Nineteenth Century* (Oxford, 1999), pp. 53–74.

38 Cooper, *Colonialism in Question*, pp. 93–110.

39 For a broader critique of the networked approach see Simon J. Potter, 'Webs, Networks, and Systems: Globalization and the Mass Media in the Nineteenth- and Twentieth-Century British Empire', *Journal of British Studies*, 46:3 (Jul. 2007), pp. 621–46.

40 Linda Colley, *Captives: Britain, Empire and the World, 1600–1850* (London, 2002), pp. 17–18.

41 Linda Colley, *The Ordeal of Elizabeth Marsh: How a Remarkable Woman Crossed Seas and Empires to Become a Part of World History* (London, 2007), pp. xiv, xxiii.

42 Ibid., p. 300.

43 Emma Rothschild, *The Inner Life of Empires: an Eighteenth-Century History* (Princeton, 2011), pp. 1–2, 6–7.

44 David Lambert and Alan Lester, 'Imperial Spaces, Imperial Subjects' in David Lambert and Alan Lester (eds), *Colonial Lives across the British Empire: Imperial Careering in the Long Nineteenth Century* (Cambridge, 2006), pp. 1–31, quote at p. 2.

45 Fedorowich and Thompson, 'Mapping the Contours of the British World', quotes at pp. 7, 15.

46 Robert Bickers, *Empire Made Me: an Englishman Adrift in Shanghai* (London, 2003), quote at p. 12.

47 Clare Anderson, *Subaltern Lives: Biographies of Colonialism in the Indian Ocean World, 1790–1920* (Cambridge, 2012).

48 See Simon J. Potter and Jonathan Saha, 'Global History, Imperial History and Connected Histories of Empire', *Journal of Colonialism and Colonial History* (forthcoming).

49 J. R. Seeley, *The Expansion of England: Two Courses of Lectures* (London, 1883), p. 10.

50 Mike Davis, *Late Victorian Holocausts: El Niño famines and the Making of the Third World* (London and New York, 2001), pp. 295, 310.

51 C. A. Bayly, 'The First Age of Global Imperialism, c.1760–1830', *Journal of Imperial and Commonwealth History*, 26:2 (May 1998), pp. 28–47, quote at p. 29.

52 Alejandro Portes, Luis E. Guarnizo, and Patricia Landolt, 'The Study of Transnationalism: Pitfalls and Promise of an Emergent Research Field', *Ethnic and Racial Studies*, 22:2 (Mar. 1999), pp. 217–37, esp. p. 227.

► Conclusions

1 In the 'Afterthoughts' written for the second edition of Ronald Robinson and John Gallagher with Alice Denny, *Africa and the Victorians: the Official Mind of Imperialism* (2nd edition, London, 1981), p. 499.

Further Reading

▶ Introduction

There are several excellent narrative and thematic accounts of the history of the British empire which can be read profitably in tandem with this book. Perhaps the most stimulating recent survey is John Darwin's *Unfinished Empire: the Global Expansion of Britain* (London, 2012). Bernard Porter's *The Lion's Share: a History of British Imperialism 1850–2011* (Harlow, 2012, 5th edition) and Ronald Hyam's *Britain's Imperial Century 1815–1914: a Study of Empire and Expansion* (Basingstoke, 2002, 3rd edition) also provide excellent overviews. Hyam's *Britain's Declining Empire: the Road to Decolonisation* (Cambridge, 2006) offers a detailed study of the official thinking behind British **decolonization**, although it is less concerned with external pressures on British decision-making, including African and Asian nationalism. The original five volumes of the *Oxford History of the British Empire* (Oxford, 1998–1999) surveyed a wide range of topics, but have been criticized for failing to consider new historiographical departures. The ever-expanding range of *Companion* volumes to the series marks an attempt to remedy this. Sarah Stockwell (ed.), *The British Empire: Themes and Perspectives* (Oxford, 2008) provides a useful set of essays on key themes. For an advanced, eclectic collection of previously published contributions to the **new imperial history** see Stephen Howe (ed.), *The New Imperial Histories Reader* (Abingdon, 2010). Howe has also written a good online essay on 'Imperial and Colonial History', available at http://www.history.ac.uk/makinghistory/resources/articles/imperial_post_colonial_history.html. For a popular attempt to highlight the positive achievements of the British empire see Niall Ferguson, *Empire: How Britain Made the Modern World* (London, 2004). John Newsinger, *The Blood Never Dried: a People's History of the British Empire* (London, 2013, new edition) offers a valuable corrective.

▶ Chapter 1: Expansion and Contraction

The classic Radical Liberal and Marxist accounts of imperialism are often still the starting point for students of the history of the British empire: see

J. A. Hobson, *Imperialism: a Study* (London, 3rd Edition, 1988 [1938]) and V. I. Lenin, *Imperialism: the Highest Stage of Capitalism* (London, 1993 [1916]). Foremost among the works that revised these older understandings is John Gallagher and Ronald Robinson, 'The Imperialism of Free Trade', *Economic History Review*, second series, 5:1 (1953), pp. 1–15, which remains essential reading. Ronald Robinson and John Gallagher with Alice Denny, *Africa and the Victorians: the Official Mind of Imperialism* (London, 2nd edition, 1981) and D. K. Fieldhouse, *Economics and Empire, 1830–1914* (London, 1973) together offer an extended and more sophisticated demolition of the received wisdom. Wm. Roger Louis and Ronald Robinson, 'The Imperialism of Decolonization', *Journal of Imperial and Commonwealth History*, 22:3 (1994), pp. 462–511 applies similar ideas to the topic of **decolonization**, with provocative results. As an attempt to return the economics of empire to centre stage, P. J. Cain and A. G. Hopkins, *British Imperialism 1688–2000* (London, 2nd Edition, 2001 [originally 2 vols, 1993]) has generated some debate, but seems to offer a less satisfactory account of imperial history than work that acknowledges the varied and divergent imperial interests of a whole range of different groups. For the most convincing pluralist accounts see C. A. Bayly, *Imperial Meridian: the British Empire and the World, 1780–1830* (London and New York, 1989) and John Darwin, *Unfinished Empire: the Global Expansion of Britain* (London, 2012).

▶ Chapter 2: Control

The literature on imperial and colonial governance and the colonial state is somewhat fragmentary. On the role of metropolitan institutions in controlling the colonies see Zoë Laidlaw, *Colonial Connections, 1815–45: Patronage, the Information Revolution and Colonial Government* (Manchester, 2005). The part played by British governors 'on the spot' in the colonies is discussed in John Benyon, 'Overlords of Empire? British "Proconsular Imperialism" in Comparative Perspective', *Journal of Imperial and Commonwealth History*, 19:2 (May 1991), pp. 164–202. For those lower down the chain of command, see Christopher Prior, *Exporting Empire: Africa, Colonial Officials and the Construction of the British Imperial State, c. 1900–1939* (Manchester, 2013). For useful introductions to the literature on the colonial state more generally see: John L. Comaroff, 'Reflections on the Colonial State, in South Africa and Elsewhere: Factions, Fragments, Facts and Fictions', *Social Identities*, 4:3 (1998), pp. 321–61; Joanna Lewis, *Empire State-Building: War and Welfare in Kenya, 1925–52* (Oxford, 2000); and Douglas M. Peers, 'State, Power, and Colonialism' in Douglas M. Peers and Nandini Gooptu (eds), *India and the British Empire* (Oxford, 2012), pp. 16–43. For the concept of **collaboration** read Anil Seal, *The Emergence of*

Indian Nationalism: Competition and Collaboration in the Later Nineteenth Century (Cambridge, 1968) and Ronald Robinson, 'Non-European Foundations of European Imperialism: Sketch for a Theory of Collaboration' in R. Owen and B. Sutcliffe (eds), *Studies in the Theory of Imperialism* (London, 1972), pp. 117–42. On theories of colonial knowledge see Bernard Cohn, *Colonialism and its Forms of Knowledge: the British in India* (Princeton, 1996) and Nicholas B. Dirks, *Castes of Mind: Colonialism and the Making of Modern India* (Princeton, 2001): for a subtle and powerful critique see C. A. Bayly, *Empire and Information: Intelligence Gathering and Social Communication in India, 1780–1870* (Cambridge, 1996).

▶ Chapter 3: Difference

Many scholars who emphasize the role of the British empire in strengthening and producing difference have drawn on Partha Chatterjee's *The Nation and its Fragments* (Princeton, 1993), and particularly his ideas about the 'rule of colonial difference'. A very useful essay that questions whether the cultural influence of empire was really transformative is Susan Bayly's 'The Evolution of Colonial Cultures: Nineteenth-Century Asia' in Andrew Porter (ed.), *The Oxford History of the British Empire* vol. III *The Nineteenth Century* (Oxford, 1999), pp. 447–69. A good introduction to the work of the Subaltern Studies school is provided by Vinayak Chaturvedi (ed.), *Mapping Subaltern Studies and the Postcolonial* (London and New York, 2000), which brings together a number of previously published articles and includes the seminal article by Ranajit Guha, 'On Some Aspects of the Historiography of Colonial India', originally published in *Subaltern Studies I: Writings on South Asian History and Society* (Delhi, 1982). The literature on empire and race is vast: for useful recent discussions see Douglas Lorimer, *Science, Race Relations and Resistance: Britain, 1870–1914* (Manchester, 2013) and the essays collected in Philip D. Morgan and Sean Hawkins (eds), *Black Experience and the Empire* (Oxford, 2004). For a similarly useful introduction to feminist histories of empire see Philippa Levine (ed.), *Gender and Empire* (Oxford, 2004).

▶ Chapter 4: Identity

J. A. Hobson has had a lasting influence over discussion of British 'popular imperialism': see in particular his book, *The Psychology of Jingoism* (London, 1901). The pioneering work in the field of the social history of the British empire was John M. MacKenzie, *Propaganda and Empire* (Manchester, 1984): see also the essays collected in John M. MacKenzie (ed.), *Imperialism and Popular Culture* (Manchester, 1986). Catherine Hall has published widely on the impact of empire on British identity and ideas about race: for the most developed statement of her views see her book *Civilising Subjects: Metropole and Colony in the English Imagination, 1830–1867* (Oxford, 2002). A very different perspective is available in Bernard Porter, *The Absent-Minded Imperialists: Empire, Society, and Culture in Britain* (Oxford, 2004). I have attempted a synthesis of debate about the impact of empire on Britain in Simon J. Potter, 'Empire, Cultures and Identities in Nineteenth- and Twentieth-Century Britain', *History Compass*, 5:1 (Jan. 2007), pp. 51–71. For broad samplings of writing on the idea of a 'British world', it is hard to better the following edited collections of essays: Carl Bridge and Kent Fedorowich (eds), *The British World: Diaspora, Culture, Identity* (London, 2003) – also available as a special issue of the *Journal of Imperial and Commonwealth History*, 31/2 (2003); Phillip Buckner and R. Douglas Francis (eds), *Rediscovering the British World* (Calgary, 2005); Phillip Buckner and R. Douglas Francis (eds), *Canada and the British World: Culture, Migration, and Identity* (Vancouver, 2005); and Kate Darien-Smith, Patricia Grimshaw, and Stuart Macintyre (eds), *Britishness Abroad: Transnational Movements and Imperial Cultures* (Melbourne, 2007).

▶ Chapter 5: Going Global

Global history has emerged as a distinct field relatively recently, and much of the most significant work on empires in global history has been published in the last 15 years. For a very readable and provocative argument about the imperial roots of modern European economic growth see Kenneth Pomeranz, *The Great Divergence: China, Europe, and the Making of the Modern World Economy* (Princeton, 2000). John Darwin's *After Tamerlane: the Global History of Empire since 1405* (London, 2007) is a crucial contribution to the field. Christopher Bayly writes about more than empire in his book *The Birth of the Modern World, 1780–1914: Global Connections and Comparisons* (Oxford, 2004), but this works to place imperial history in some unfamiliar and thought-provoking contexts. On the concept of imperial webs and networks see Tony Ballantyne, *Orientalism and Race: Aryanism in the British Empire* (Basingstoke, 2002) and Alan Lester, 'British Settler Discourse and the Circuits of Empire', *History Workshop Journal*, 54 (Autumn 2002), pp. 24–48. For attempts to write global lives see Linda Colley's two books, *Captives: Britain, Empire and the World, 1600–1850* (London, 2002) and *The Ordeal of Elizabeth Marsh: How a Remarkable Woman Crossed Seas and Empires to Become a Part of World History* (London, 2007), Emma Rothschild's *The Inner Life of Empires: an Eighteenth-Century History* (Princeton, 2011), Clare Anderson's, *Subaltern Lives: Biographies of Colonialism in the Indian Ocean World, 1790–1920* (Cambridge, 2012), and Robert Bickers' *Empire Made Me: an Englishman Adrift in Shanghai* (London, 2003).

Newport Community
Learning & Libraries

Index